WALKING in EDEN
Circular and Linear Routes in the Eden Valley

Ron Scholes

Published by Sigma Leisure – an imprint of
Sigma Press, 5 Alton Road, Wilmslow, Cheshire SK9 5DY, England.

British Library Cataloguing in Publication Data
A CIP record for this book is available from the British Library.

ISBN: 1-85058-836-8

Typesetting and Design by: Sigma Press, Wilmslow, Cheshire.

Cover photograph: view to Wild Boar Fell from Pendragon Castle

Maps and photographs: Ron Scholes

Printed by: Bell & Bain Ltd, Glasgow

Disclaimer: the information in this book is given in good faith and is believed to be correct at the time of publication. No responsibility is accepted by either the author or publisher for errors or omissions, or for any loss or injury howsoever caused. Only you can judge your own fitness, competence and experience. Do not rely solely on sketch maps for navigation: we strongly recommend the use of appropriate Ordnance Survey (or equivalent) maps.

Preface

Section 1

The cradle of Eden lies in the wild and rugged hills of upper Mallerstang. The river rises on Blackfell Moss below Hugh's Seat, and flows through a limestone chasm to reach a fine waterfall before turning northwards on its sedate journey of 75 miles (120km) to the sea. The high hills on either side of the dale rise to over 2,000 feet, culminating in Wild Boar Fell, 2,324ft (708m) and High Seat, 2,326ft (709m).

The Settle-Carlisle railway, road and river all run through the Mallerstang parallel to each other. Along the valley bottom, farmsteads are scattered in splendid isolation among the patches of pasture and woodland enlivening the barren landscape.

The Howgill Fells are quite unlike the craggy mountains of Lakeland. The basic rocks of these hills belong to the Silurian period, and mainly consist of a resistant grey sandstone of the type known as Coniston grit. Glacial action has caused smooth slopes and rounded summits, and the central area constitutes an undulating plateau from which grassy ridges radiate like the spokes of a wheel.

Section 2

To the west of Kirkby Stephen, there are rivers and streams that, geographically speaking, belong to the Eden such as Helm Beck, Hoff Beck and Lyvennet Beck. The valley of the Lyvennet Beck lies in a shallow depression in an elevated plateau. The river gently meanders from an upland of bare limestone, to richer pastures and woods on a bedrock of red sandstone. This is an area of farmsteads and sleepy hamlets, where the walking is on velvet turf alongside crystal-clear watercourses.

A survey of prehistoric habitation sites on the limestone uplands after five years of fieldwalking, threw some light on the origins and living practices of the prehistoric inhabitants of this north west corner of England.

The town of Brough lies at the foot of the Pennine slopes, and guards the ancient route over Stainmore. The stark ruins of Brough Castle occupy a dominant position overlooking Swindale Beck. The fortress was built by the Normans on the site of the Roman fort of *Verterae*.

A short distance to the west, the River Eden bends northwards. Close by lies the peaceful village of Great Musgrave, noted for its ancient rush-bearing ceremony.

Section 3

The river Eden loops round the historic town of Appleby, now properly called Appleby-in-Westmorland and commemorating a link with its former status as a county town. Amongst many attractive features are the handsome thoroughfare of Boroughgate, the parish church of St Lawrence, the well-preserved castle and the fine sandstone bridge spanning the river.

As it travels northwards the Eden passes through gentle pastoral country, patterned by hedgerows, copses of woodland and rich arable land with its fields of dark red soil. Paths, tracks and country lanes link together the vale's rural settlements.

East of Penrith, the Eden follows a course regarded by many as its most

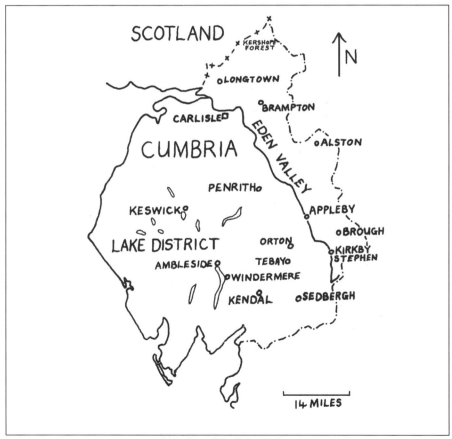

Location of the Eden Valley

beautiful stretch. The river runs through a red sandstone gorge with turbulent water amongst beautiful wooded scenery.

Interesting features at Wetheral include St Constantine's Cells cut into the sandstone cliff, the well-preserved gatehouse of a Benedictine priory and the high railway bridge across the river which supports a cast-iron footbridge.

Section 4

On the eastern fellsides, villages and hamlets lie beside swift-flowing streams that race down to meet the main river. The surroundings illustrate a complete canvas of high fells with rocky faces, moorland ridges and upland pastures. The stout stone dwellings were built to resist border incursions by the Scots, as well as defying the temperamental local weather.

The Pennine moorlands are a wild landscape of rough grass and heather, patches of bilberry and cotton grass, with stone-littered slopes, and extensive areas where the poorly aerated ground gives rise to deep peat deposits.

Another interesting feature is the stratum of exposed igneous rock; a hard black quartz dolerite material known as the Whin Sill. High Cup Gill is a spectacular, deep, crag-rimmed hollow where this volcanic intrusion rims the cliffs of a long glaciated side valley of the Eden. The High Cup Scar is remarkable for the evenness of its upper layer of crags which extend in a horseshoe round the dale head.

Section 5

Finally, the Eden leaves the high hills behind and is joined by the lively Rivers Gelt and Irthing. Both valleys retain evidence of the presence of the Roman occupation of our land.

As the river passes by the City of Carlisle, the visitor may well be advised to spend time looking at some of its attractions: the Cathedral, the Tullie House Museum and its superb collection of Roman material, the Art Gallery, and Carlisle Castle with its Museum to The King's Own Border Regiment.

Beyond the urban fringe the Eden wriggles briefly though open countryside, as the walking route follows the line of Hadrian's Wall. Soon the river reaches the wide mudflats and sandy wastes of the Solway Firth.

The area north-east of Carlisle is an attractive mixture of rolling countryside dotted with remote farms and settlements, culminating in the vast tracts of afforestation along the border with Scotland. This relatively unknown region of north east Cumbria, from the usual tourist point of view, is a landscape just waiting to be explored.

Eden Benchmark Sculptures

A sculpture collection to celebrate the River Eden was commissioned to mark the new millennium by East Cumbria Countryside Project and local communities along the river. The sculptures fulfil a dual function of landmarks and seats and are located on or near to many of the walks in this book:

Section 1

Walk: Mallerstang Heights and Edenside
Sculpture: 'Water Cut' by Mary Bourne
Location: Lady Anne Clifford's Way, Mallerstang
Map reference: SD 786 985 OS OL 19; Landranger No. 98

Walk: High Pike Hill and Nine Standards Rigg
Sculpture: 'Passage' by Laura White
Location: Stenkrith Park, Kirkby Stephen. Slight deviation from route of walk; approached by path on west bank of River Eden.
Map reference: NY 774 075 OS OL 19; Landranger No. 91.

Section 3

Walk: Appleby: riverside and pastureland paths to a fine waterfall
Sculpture: 'Primrose Stone' by Joss Smith
Location: near Bongate Mill, Appleby, close to start of walk.
Map reference: NY 687 199 OS OL 19; Landranger No.91

Walk: Glassonby: an historical exploration – a bastle, a castle, caves and a stone circle.
Sculpture: 'Cypher Piece' by Frances Pelly
Location: Eden Bridge, Lazonby. Close to Eden Bridge on west bank of River Eden.
Map reference: NY 549 402, OS OL5; Landranger No. 86

Walk: Armathwaite and along the bank of the River Eden
Sculpture: 'Flight of Fancy' by Tim Shutter
Location: near church, Wetheral
Map reference: NY 468 543, OS Explorer No. 315; Landranger No. 86

Section 5

Walk: Carlisle and Hadrian's Wall
Sculpture: 'Towards the Sea' by Hideo Furuta
Location: North of castle, Carlisle. Close to start of walk
Map reference: NY 397 566 OS Explorer No. 315, Landranger No. 85

Other Sculpture Locations

Sculpture: 'Red River' by Victoria Brailsford
Location: West View Farm, Temple Sowerby
Map reference: 605 275 OS OL19; Landranger No. 91

Sculpture: 'South Rising' by Vivien Mousdell
Location: Ladies Walk, Edenhall
Map reference: 569 326 OS OL5; Landranger No. 90

Sculpture: 'Visa' by Graeme Mitcheson
Location: Coombs Week, Armathwaite
Map reference: 507 451 OS OL5; Landranger No. 86

Sculpture: 'Global Warning' by Anthony Turner
Location: Village Green, Rockcliffe
Map reference: 357 617 OS Explorer 315; Landranger No. 85

Notes

In the information panel at the beginning of each walk:

Distance also states whether the route is circular or linear.

The heading **Maps** indicates the sheets required: for example 1:25000 Explorer, 2½ inches to the mile. These are identified by a sheet number and a national grid reference, thus: OS OL19 NY/SD. The 1:25,000 sheets are recommended for walking as they include such invaluable detail as field boundaries. Also, the 1:50,000 Landranger OS maps at a scale of 1¼ inches to the mile. These are identified by a reference number, for example: Landranger 91. They indicate walking routes, as well as giving a good overall picture of a particular area. However, they do not include the same amount of detail as the Explorer series.

Note: The letters WM in the text indicate Way Marker and BW, bridleway.

Linear and Link-up Walks

Linear walks, unlike circular perambulations, depend on local transport such as buses or trains, for the return journey. Otherwise, vehicle support has to be organised.

Some short linear walks are included to enable other routes to be linked together or to give alternatives. Examples of such walks are:

Garsdale Head to Ravenstonedale, pages 29-38, Section 1

Great Asby, Asby Gill, Gaythorne, Gaythorne Plain, pages 51-57, Section 2

Appleby to Dufton, pages 76-80, Section 3

Route Advice

The routes described present no technical difficulties in good summer weather, and indeed the majority may also be completed in good winter conditions. However, for those routes that proceed across the Pennine moorlands, one should be aware of the problems caused by mist and should be proficient in map and compass skills. In snow and ice conditions, wear the correct clothing, carry food and warm drinks, and remember that an ice axe is an essential item of equipment.

Contents

Section 4: The Pennines

Section 5: North Eden

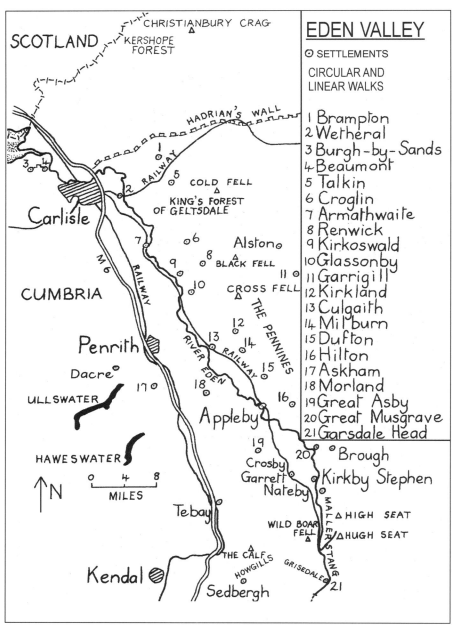

Locations of Walks

Section 1: The Mallerstang Area

The name 'Mallerstang' is sometimes interpreted as Mallard Stank or Stang; the pool of the wild duck. But it is more likely to be identified with *mellor*, or the Welsh equivalent *Moelfre*, a bare hill. The word *Stang* or *Stong* is the Old Norse for a pole or a boundary marker.

The more subdued type of topography in the south of Lakeland continues to the east in the Howgill Fells. These smooth grassy hills are underlain by resistant grey sandstone of the Silurian Period, known as Coniston Grit. The Howgill Fells constitute superb walking country, an undulating plateau with radiating ridges, smooth slopes, rounded summits and steep sided valleys.

The Mallerstang area is different in character and more akin to the Pennines. Here, the underlying rocks consist of sandstone, shale and layers of Great Scar Limestone. The higher hills are capped with millstone grit, with Wild Boar Fell, 2323ft (708m) thrusting its rocky face above a limestone plateau pitted with shake holes.

The River Eden rises on Black Fell Moss below Hugh Seat as Red Gill. It is believed that when the Mallerstang was gouged out during the Ice Ages, the deposits of material caused the stream to flow south-west and then northwards. This meant that Red Gill was originally a tributary of the Ure.

Between the Howgill Fells and the Mallerstang lies the remote valley of Grisedale. Enclosed by the sprawling slopes of Baugh Fell and Swarth Fell, this green depression amidst the hills is drained by many streams. Near Uldale the lively River Rawthey cuts through beds of limestone creating beautiful waterfalls.

The Settle to Carlisle railway runs through the Mallerstang. The building of the whole line from Settle to Carlisle took six years, through very difficult terrain. It was opened for passenger traffic in May 1876. The railway, road and river all run through the dale parallel to each other. Scattered farmsteads are dotted along the valley bottom and on the lower slopes. Some dwellings give clues as to their early Norse beginnings: Angerholm – fertile meadow, Ais Gill – water gill, Hanging Lund – a wood on the side of a hill.

History has touched the dale in the form of the Kaber Rigg Plot. In April 1663, a plot was hatched to raise an armed force to compel Charles II to grant religious toleration to all except Roman Catholics and to do away with all taxes. Robert Atkinson of Dalefoot, agreed to raise a force of a hundred or so armed men. But the support was not forthcoming and the insurrection was ended. However, Atkinson was gaoled, escaped and then gave himself up. Ultimately, he was sentenced to be hung, drawn and quartered. Sadly, a warrant to reprieve Atkinson did not reach Appleby until he was dead.

The busy market town of Kirkby Stephen lies where the valley of the Eden broadens out after its journey through the narrow Mallerstang. The varied nature of the surrounding scenery attracts many visitors, particularly walkers engaged on the Coast to Coast journey from St Bees to Robin Hood's Bay. No doubt they look forward to climbing the Pennine escarpment and the summit of Nine Standards Rigg.

Cotegill and Wild Boar Fell

Route: Cotegill Bridge, Aisgill Moor Cottages, Stubbing Rigg, Swarth
                      Fell Pike, Swarth Fell, Fell Tarn, High White Scar, Wild Boar
                      Fell, The Nab, High Dolphinsty, Hazel Gill, Ing Heads, Hanging
                      Lund, Slade Edge, Hellgill Force, Aisgill Moor Cottages,
                      Cotegill Bridge.

Distance: 9½ miles (15.2km) circular walk

Highest Elevation: Wild Boar Fell 2,324ft (708m)

Total ascent: 1,827ft (557m)

Maps: 1:25000 Explorer OL No.19; 1:50000 Landranger No. 98.

How to get there: Take B6259 road north from Moorcock Inn – (A684) or, south
                      from Kirkby Stephen.

Start/finish point: Cotegill Bridge; grid reference SD 7740 9690

Terrain: Moorland slopes and hill ridges. Pleasant valley paths.

From almost any angle in the Mallerstang Valley or from the eastern escarpment edges of High Pike Hill, High Seat and Hangingstone Scar, the magnificent thrusting summit of Wild Boar Fell commands one's attention; its rocky
face rising above a limestone plateau scarred by shake holes. However, not
to be outdone, and an integral part of the scene, are its neighbours Little Fell
and Swarth Fell. These outlying hills can also be part of a more challenging
circuit of the valley heights. Another lovely approach is a splendid walk
across the limestone Stennerskeugh Clouds and via High Greenrigg and
lonely Sand Tarn to the summit of Wild Boar Fell. Whether half-hidden in
mist like a Chinese watercolour painting, covered in snow or bathed in
sunshine, Wild Boar Fell has that little extra bit of mountain magic.

The more subdued type of topography in the south of Lakeland continues
to the east in the Howgill Fells, until the flat stony top of Wild Boar Fell indicates that pre-Carboniferous rocks have been replaced by a cap of millstone
grit. In fact, this same geological sequence is continued over the High Seat,
High Pike and Nine Standards Rigg route; that is, alternating layers of Great
Scar Limestone, with younger limestones and millstone grits.

During the Ice Age, the Mallerstang was a high plateau beneath the
glacier. The glacial activity was divided into four periods separated by warm
inter-glacial times. It is interesting to note that when the Mallerstang was
gouged out, some geologists believe that deposits of material caused Red Gill
Beck, the source of the River Eden, to flow south-west and then northwards.
So that Hell Gill Beck was formerly a feeder of the Ure.

Intake to Wild Boar Fell

The Walk

From a small parking area by Cotegill Bridge walk along the road to Aisgill
Moor Cottages. Take the start of the public bridleway to Grisedale, then
immediately head on a direct course up the grassy slopes of Stubbing Rigg;
along the line on paper, of the North Yorkshire/Cumbria border. The ridge is
easily reached near the south cairn on Swarth Fell Pike. Bear right and
follow the fence passing two more cairns. Note the circular O.S. Survey Plate
in the ground, and over the fence on the left is a cairn and trig point. From
here there are fine views of the Howgill Fells, Baugh Fell, Grisedale, and in
the distance the hazy forms of Whernside and Ingleborough. Continue along
the right-hand side of the fence passing a small pool in a dip and gradually
ascend the fellside. At the crest of the slope a wall comes in at right angles
but keep straight on following the wall to the ridge top, which is now littered
with stones and boulders.

The summit cairn of Swarth Fell, 2234 ft (681m) lies to the right. Ahead,
the cairns on the south end of Wild Boar Fell come into view. Descend gently
at first, then more steeply on grass with more lovely views of the Howgill
Fells. Walk down to a wet area with an elongated pool, where its dark peaty
waters are frequently ruffled by the wind; a lonely and evocative place. Note:

This little tarn is not named on the OS maps. So the author has taken the liberty of giving it the name of Fell Tarn.

From the col climb easily up the grassy slopes ahead and slant to the right. The gradient levels out and ends with a pleasant walk to a stile over a fence, before reaching a rash of cairns on the edge of the escarpment. This is the better viewpoint as it commands a superb view of the Mallerstang Valley. The cairns have sprung up here due to the availability of loose stone lying about the surface. They provide little shelter, but there are one or two ground hollows to curl up in out of the wind.

The true summit of Wild Boar Fell, 2,324ft (708m) lies on a north-westerly bearing, a short walk across the flat top. There is an OS Survey Column and a stone shelter. From the summit, walk just east of north-east to reach The Nab. The route from the rash of cairns lies along the escarpment edge to arrive at The Nab.

At this point, the slopes fall steeply away; a mass of tumbled rocks, boulders and scree. This is another magnificent viewpoint down the dale.

Descend steeply following the escarpment edge to reach the angle of a wall coming in from the left. Turn sharp right, the location marked on the map as High Dolphinsty and descend into a dip. The path traverses against the slope and veers towards a limestone pavement. Here the route becomes indistinct, but make your way over the limestone pasture keeping to the left and below this little plateau. Cross the boundary line beyond Little Wold and descend the grassy slope to a gate in a fence. There's a ruined building in front, bear right by a wall and notice the little waterfall down below in the gully to the right – this is a glorious spot for forty winks!

Pass through a gap in the wall and cross the stream, and then walk on the track past a barn. Proceed ahead through another wall gap, as the track swings to the left and passes under the Settle to Carlisle railway line. Carry on through a gap in a wall and descend to Hazelgill Farm. Keep right and aim for a metal gate in the corner, and go across the meadow to a stile in the wall. Walk through a pine copse to a wall stile and proceed along the river bank. The way lies through a flower-bedecked meadow before reaching a bridge. Cross over the River Eden to meet the road and footpath sign. There's another footpath sign on the far side, so slant right towards a stile in the wall. Cross a farm track and walk across a pasture towards a partially blocked stile. Note, there is a gate further on along the wall.

Aim for the top left-hand corner of the field towards a building and to a stile in the wall. Pass in front of the building and head half left towards a gate and a step stile in a wall, having passed through an area of young trees. Continue just to the right of an electricity pole to a gap stile in a wall. Carry on across the meadow guided by a helpful yellow plastic bucket lid indicating the step stile in the wall.

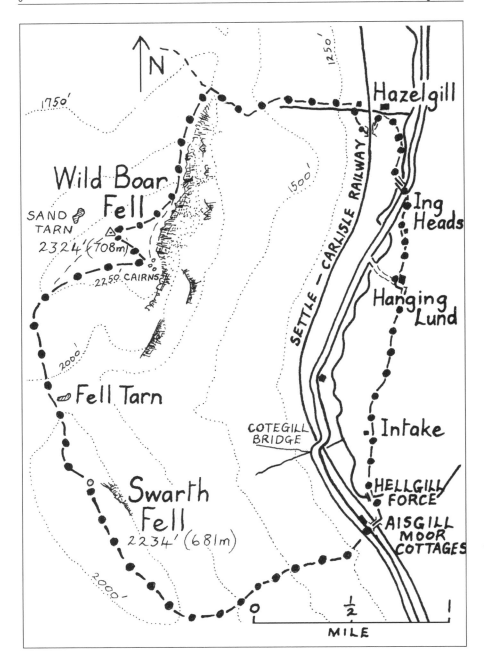

From here proceed in front of Hanging Lund Farm to reach a gate with a way marker. Cross the stream over a footbridge to a gate with a footpath sign. Bear left, follow the wall to a gate with a PUBLIC BRIDLEWAY sign, and head up the walled grassy way which is boggy in places.

Hanging Lund Farm was originally two houses, as many of the dwellings in the dale seem to date from the seventeenth century, when much re-building was carried out after the Civil War. The walls are of rubble with a slate roof, though originally, the farm would have a thatched roof. In 1829, Hanging Lund was called a hamlet, and as with many houses in the dale, peat was burned on the fires. The cutting of peat took place on the fellsides above Hanging Lund, and probably the fires were not allowed to go out because of the difficulty of re-lighting with a tinderbox.

Continue up to a gate which has a 'Beware of the Bull' sign on its reverse side. There is a barn ahead as the way follows the wall, and starts to climb passing a small quarry working to reach a gateway. Beyond this gate DO NOT follow the faint grooved track up the slope, but continue straight on across the grassy slope to meet a gap in a wall. Pass a spring issuing from a small limestone outcrop and follow the wall to a gate by a small clump of sycamore trees. Proceed along Slade Edge, a limestone terrace, with good views down the dale, and carry on alongside the wall. The building, Intake, lies to the right as the path reaches a step stile.

Walk along the access track to a gate, and on to another gate by a corrugated iron shed. The route crosses Hell Gill Beck and it's worth a minute or two admiring nearby Hellgill Force. This fine waterfall plunges 60ft (18.28m) over a limestone scar, as the Hell Gill Beck is about to change direction from south-west to north.

The track carries on crossing over the railway line before joining the road at Aisgill Moor Cottages. Turn right and stroll down the road to the starting point at Cotegill Bridge.

Aisgill, Lunds:
a watershed walk through upland dales

Route:	Aisgill Moor Cottages, Grisedale Common, Garsdale Head, South Lunds, Lunds, River Ure, Aisgill Moor Cottages.
Distance:	7 miles (11.2km) circular walk.
Highest Elevation:	Grisedale Common 1,516ft (462m)
Total Ascent:	676ft (206m)
Maps:	1:25000 Explorer OL No. 19; 1:50000 Landranger No. 98
How to get there:	Take the B6259 road north from Moorcock Inn (A684) or, south from Kirkby Stephen.
Start/Finish Point:	Aisgill Moor Cottages, grid reference SD 778 963
Terrain:	Moorland slopes and upland river pastures

The two famous northern rivers, the Ure and the Eden have their sources close together on the high moors in Upper Mallerstang. The Eden turns north, and flows into the Solway; the Clough River flows westwards down Garsdale, and the Ure flows eastwards down Wensleydale.

The Walk

Leave the road at Aisgill Moor Cottages where there is a WM to Grisedale. Go through a gate, and slant left alongside a fence to reach a gate in corner of walls. Put on your dark glasses and ignore a 'Beware of the Bull' sign, and proceed on a faint path across a rough grassy fellside. As the wall on the right bends away, approach a gate. Continue to follow the wall on your left to reach another gate in the corner of a wall. Maintain your way along the faint path alongside the wall, and arrive at the ruined farm of High Shaw Paddock. There is a fine barn here, and also a large wild cherry tree. Cameras should be at the ready, as this is an ideal location for superb views down the dale.

Slant to the right and head across to a gap in the wall; then walk forward up the sloping meadow to a small gate and gap stile bearing a WM. Continue to ascend across Rowan Tree Side over rough moor grass and rushes. Aim for a small nick in the hill ridge; this feature is on a line with the rail tunnel and plantation in the valley below. Another useful guide for your position is that a wall climbing up from the valley makes a sharp left-angled turn. There is a gate and a fence ahead. From the wall corner walk ahead over the moor and descend towards the distant Butterbeck Plantation in Grisedale. Aim for the wall in the immediate foreground on an intermittent path, and bear right

Garsdale station

along the track. The track meets a small road that descends towards East House.

Approach a gate, and the road eventually becomes fully metalled. Continue down the road to Moor Rigg, with a gate just before the farm. Bear left just after the building, WM Garsdale Head. Go across the meadow to a stile in the wall, and then keep to the right of a barn on a clear path. Walk down the meadow towards the ruinous building of Rowantree, and on through a stile, WM. Use the stone slabs to cross a watercourse, and gently ascend the slope to reach a stile in a wall. Proceed past a barn on the left to a stile, descend briefly to cross a small watercourse, and walk ahead to a gap stile and gate in wall corner. Bear right, pass the building of Blake Mire, and proceed across the moor grass with electricity pylons to the left. In the middle distance ahead is a view of Garsdale Station on the Settle-Carlisle line. Immediately to the right, the steep slopes tumble down to Grisedale Beck. Follow a clear path in grassy surroundings to a stile, WM. Descend, and follow a stone wall to a gap stile and gate, WM, to reach the A684. Garsdale station lies just ahead along the minor road.

Turn left, and walk along the main road for a short distance. Opposite to a line of cottages there is a step gap stile with a gate, WM , to South Lunds; a route across Garsdale Low Moor. Aim for a gap in a wall and continue slant-

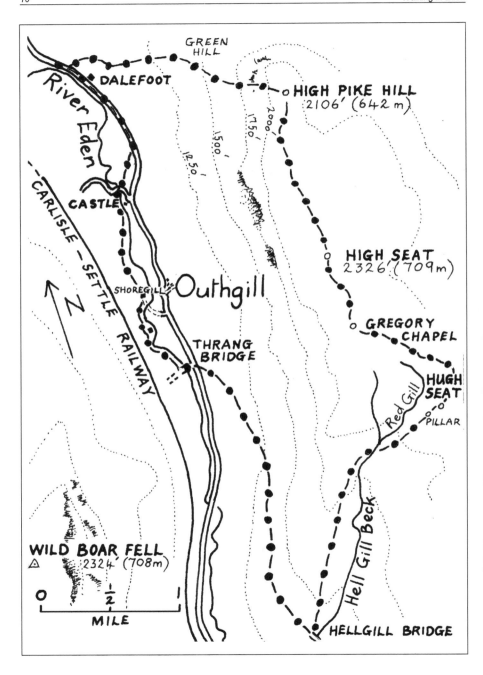

ing partly right. The way climbs gently again with a fairly clear path on the ground to reach a gap stile. From this point there is a view of Dandrymire Viaduct, and the line of the old railway track bed into Wensleydale.

NOTE: The Wensleydale Railway Association already run services in the dale from Leeming Bar to Redmire, with station stops at Bedale, Finghall and Leyburn. Their ultimate aim is to open the whole route from Northallerton to Garsdale. Internet Site: www.wensleydalerailway.com

Walk on across the moor to reach a ladder stile over a wall, with a view of the Eden Valley. Make for the right-hand side of the house, South Lunds, and the footbridge over the railway. Descend a short, steep grassy slope and through an area of rushy pasture to a step gap stile. Cross over the footbridge, and walk across the field to a gap stile and small gate in the wall, WM.

Cross over the road, the B6259, to a gap stile and gate in the wall to the right of a house, WM. Go on for a few paces to a gate in the wall, and aim for a barn ahead. There is a section of poor, rushy pasture to negotiate, then a descent to cross a small watercourse. Proceed up to a gap stile in the wall to the left of the barn. Slant across the rough pasture on the same heading to Blades Footbridge over the River Ure. Walk straight ahead to a gate, and then alongside a fence, and continue to a step stile in the corner of a wall and fence. Turn left and accompany the wall to cross a watercourse, and walk towards a step stile in a wall. Ascend the slope ahead to a step gap stile in a wall, and continue over gentle Cowshaw Hill. Pass through a gap stile with gate in the wall, WM, and walk into the old burial ground at Lunds.

Close to the tiny, forlorn chapel are some weather-beaten gravestones, dated, 1795, 1840 and 1870; such as Catherine, Daughter of John and Isabella Blades, who died April 22nd 1844, aged 24 years. The rather sad building stands at 1066ft (325m) above sea level, and was closed many years ago.

Continue to a gap stile and gate in the wall, and walk over a footbridge across the beck to a gate, WM, into a track. Proceed straight on to a gate and enter a walled trackway. The route continues straight on through a wall stile, across rough pasture to a stone step stile

The white-painted house, called Shaws, higher up the hillside, once a much – loved youth hostel, was formerly the home of Robert Andrew Scott Macfie; a Liverpool business man and a former editor of the Gypsy Lore Journal. He is remembered in the dale as the man who paid for the services of lecturers to visit this isolated farming community. The speakers arrived by train in winter time, and talked to the local farmers on methods of improving their rough pasture land. R A Scott Macfie died in 1935, and is buried in Lunds churchyard.

Walk ahead towards a stone barn set amongst old pasture that needs draining and improving. Approach a gate and walk to the barn. Pass through a gate, cross a watercourse, and continue across improved pasture to a gate. Keep on the same heading across a large field to another gate. Aim for the barn ahead, an attractive building, and continue to the farmhouse at Low West End. Proceed through a gap stile and down to the farm track. Pass the house and stone buildings after turning left, and go through a gate on the right; this is on a short length of track across the beck. Walk to the left down the rough pastureland to a step stile in the far corner ahead. Bear left down the track to a gate, and meet the stone-arched How Beck Bridge that spans the Ure.

Turn right immediately over the bridge to the corner of a stone wall, and go through a gate with an old metal railway notice – FASTEN GATE. Turn left up alongside the wall, then bear slightly right, and walk towards a wall with a step stile. There are steps down to cross the railway: STOP, LOOK, LISTEN – BEWARE OF TRAINS

On the other side of the railway tracks, ascend to a step stile in the wall, and continue diagonally to the right. Cross a water course and walk towards a barn and house by the B6259 road. Turn right for a short walk back to the starting point at Aisgill Moor Cottages.

Mallerstang Heights and Edenside

Route: Dalefoot, Fair Hill, High Pike, High Seat, Gregory Chapel, Hugh Seat, Red Gill, High Rigg, Hell Gill Bridge, The High Way, Thrang Bridge, Shoregill, Castle Bridge, Dalefoot

Distance: 12½ miles (20km) circular walk

Highest Elevation: High Seat, 2326ft (709m)

Total ascent: 1725ft (534m)

Maps: 1:25000 Explorer OL No.19; 1:50000 Landranger Nos 91, 98

How to get there: From the north, A685 Kirkby Stephen, then B6259 via Nateby. From the south, A684 Moorcock Inn, then B6259 via Outhgill

Start/finish point: Dalefoot grid reference NY 7813 0435

Terrain: Grassy slopes, moorland escarpment; rough, peaty and stony ground, contrasting valley walk. Note: In misty weather conditions, map reading and compass skills needed on high level section.

The Walk

At Dalefoot the River Eden runs close to the road and ample parking may be found on the large, open grassy area. Bear right along the road and note the footpath sign on the left by the wall. Proceed to a stile in the fence and follow the wall round to the right. Where the track bifurcates bear left uphill towards Long Crag Quarry. Zigzag to the right to follow a faint path and then continue to ascend the grassy slope. To the right is a gully with a lining of boulders and a ruined barn. A more distinct section of path approaches the corner of a wall with a tree and a patch of rushes.

At this point strike off to the left up the pathless grassy slopes of Fair Hill and aim for two stone pillars on the skyline – not the top! Look back for rewarding views across the valley to Wild Board Fell, Swarth Fell and the Howgills. Cross a small streamlet and note the road to the north snaking over to Swaledale. Ascend steeply through an area littered with good roofing stone around the disused quarry workings and continue up the grassy slopes ahead.

Proceed across the flat ridge top of Fells End, complete with small pools, and bear right along the path to a cairn on High Pike, 2,106ft (642m). The way climbs almost imperceptibly across peaty ground and past a cairn set on a bouldery slope. Walk over grass to the next cairn, as the land in front falls away to reveal a magnificent view of the valley and its bordering escarpment

The Thrang, Upper Eden Valley

edges. The land also inclines to the east, but in a gentler fashion; it falls away like a russet-coloured sea towards the headwaters of the River Swale.

Go forward on a grassy surface to reach a stone standing on its end and a large cairn set on a rocky bed – the summit of High Seat, 2,326ft (709m). The pile of stones provides some shelter in a rather exposed situation and, as a matter of interest, just pips Wild Boar Fell by one metre.

Aim half-left towards the next cairn, passing Steddale Mouth and proceed across moorland littered by outcropping stones. The next landmark is a tall slender column of fine stonework accompanied by a circular shelter – a useful windbreak and a more comfortable butty stop. This location is grandly called 'Gregory Chapel'.

The area beyond consists of broken ground and the path becomes indistinct in places. Keep to the left-hand edge of a small ridge and head for a cairn set on a rise. There are also two tallish cairns beyond near to the fence, which is the country boundary between Cumbria and Yorkshire. Follow the fence as it swings to the west and on to the next top, which is the summit of Hugh Seat 2,260ft (689m). The name perpetuates the memory of Sir Hugh de Morville, one of the knights involved in the murder of Thomas a Becket the Archbishop of Canterbury in 1170. The knights acted on Henry II's angry cry, 'Who will rid me of this turbulent priest?'.

Mallerstang Edge also commemorates another famous owner of the

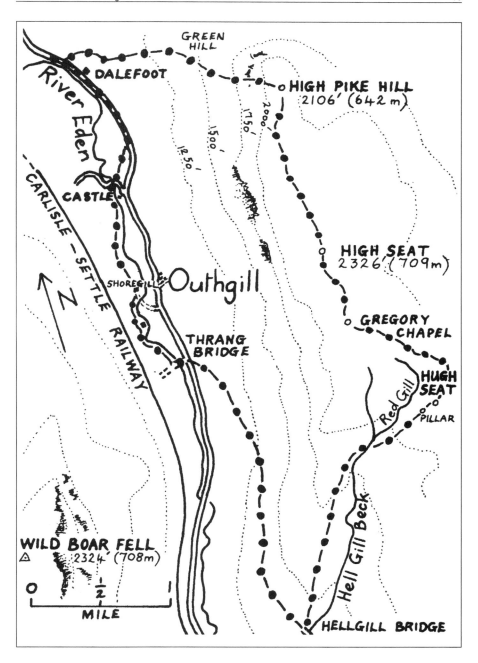

Manor of Mallerstang, in the redoubtable personage of Lady Anne Clifford, Countess of Dorset and Pembroke. Continue beyond the west end of the fence to reach a squared-off cairn with inscribed stones on its east and west sides. On the eastern side, FHL 180, and on the western face, AP 1664 – this is Lady's Pillar, Anne Clifford's boundary stone.

Head in a westerly direction downslope to a cairn and aim for another cairn beyond which is set on a little rise. This is a rough section to negotiate, in the form of thick tussocky grass, heather and bilberry, that conceal hollows in the uneven surface of the ground. Cross the stream Red Gill, the source of the River Eden, and make for a ruined structure under the lee of the ridge. Ascend the slope, now easier going underfoot, and pick up a faint track on High Rigg. Bear left and descend easily in line with a building in the middle distance. A plantation to the left enclosed by a stone wall marks the course of Hell Gill Beck. At Hell Gill Bridge, spare a moment or two peering down into limestone depths of the chasm.

The narrow bridge over the gorge is part of an ancient route, The High Way, linking Wensleydale and Mallerstang; it was no doubt used by Lady Anne Clifford on coach journeys between her various castles.

From Hell Gill Bridge walk north along the pleasant track gradually descending with recurring views of the valley and its craggy escarpment edges. On reaching the B6259 road walk for a few paces and then turn left down the track to Thrang Bridge. Cross the bridge, turn right and walk alongside the river to a step stile in a wall. Continue on the riverbank through the meadow to reach a gate. Pass by Mallerstang Farm with outbuildings on the left to meet a farm lane. Bear left to an arrow marker on a post and cross the pasture to a gap stile in a wall. Beyond the river to the right lies St Mary's Church, Outhgill. The path continues through a lovely leafy area to join a track leading to a bridge crossing the Eden. Turn left along the track, and then go through a metal gate on the right into the farmyard at Shoregill. Note that the modernised building on the left is the village Post Office.

Proceed through a gap, follow a meadowside wall to a gate and cross a small field to a gap stile in a wall edged with red paint. Make for a red painted step stile, then a tree displaying a red marker and ascend to another red coloured metal ladder over a fence. Cross a small stream gully and pass to the right of a ruined barn standing in a rushy meadow. Head for a step stile in a wall, cross a stream and pass by another barn.

At this point the river flows through more leafy surroundings and is flanked by meadows profusely decorated with many varieties of wild flowers – a gorgeous sight. On the far bank of the river lie the ruined walls of Pendragon Castle, which have undergone stabilisation work.

N.B. Some notes on the history of the castle may be found in the text of 'The Castles of Upper Eden' walk.

Follow a paddock fence to reach Castle Bridge. Turn right and then take the path on the left. From the stone step-stile, cross the riverside meadow to another stile. Ascend the slope and pass to the left of a roofless barn to meet a gate and a wall stile. Continue across the pasture to a stile in a short section of wall and proceed in the same direction to reach a gate access to the B6259 road. Bear left and walk for three quarters of a mile back to the starting point.

High Pike Hill and Nine Standards Rigg

Route:	Kirkby Stephen, Nateby, Great Bell, Green Hill, Fair Hill, High Pike Hill, Lamps Moss, Rollinson Gill, Nine Standards Rigg, Nine Standards Stones, Hartley Fell, Hartley, Kirkby Stephen
Distance:	12 miles (19.2km) circular walk
Highest Elevation:	2172ft (662m)
Total ascent:	2096ft (639m)
Maps:	1:25000 Explorer OL No.19; 1:50000 Landranger O.S. No. 91
How to get there:	M6 Junction 38, then A685 to Kirkby Stephen M6 junction 37, then A684 to Sedbergh and A683 to Kirkby Stephen, A66 to Brough-Under-Stainmore, then A685 to Kirkby Stephen
Start/finish point:	Kirkby Stephen grid reference NY 7750 0865
Terrain:	Grassy slopes and high moorland. Some peaty sections and limestone pavements. Note: There is a request to walkers from the National Park Officer, Yorkshire Dales National Park, to help prevent path erosion from Nine Standards Rigg to Kirkby Stephen. A scheme called 'Route of the Season' has been introduced in order to minimise the risk of damage to the deep peat areas and its vulnerable vegetation.

Green Route: B6270, Lamps Moss to Hartley Fell, for use from December to April. **Red and Blue Routes:** Nine Standards Rigg, Nine Standards Stones to Hartley Fell. For use May to November. **Green, Red and Blue routes:** Hartley Fell to Kirkby Stephen. For use December to November.

The name Kirkby Stephen is derived from the Old Norse Kirkiubyr and means 'a village with a church'. In 1090-7 it was known as Cherkaby Stephan, and as Kircabi Stephan in 1157.

The busy market town lies where the valley of the River Eden broadens out after its journey through the narrow Mallerstang. It is the commercial centre for a large agricultural district and is situated on one of the main routes from the north-east to the Lancashire holiday resorts and the Lake District. The varied nature of the surrounding hill and river valley scenery has meant a welcome increase in tourist traffic; the town is a popular stopping-off point on Wainright's Coast to Coast walking route, with numerous accommodation facilities.

The wide main street has a number of narrow ways leading from the thoroughfare; culminating in the Market Place facing the entrance to the church. Here, there is the notable pillared cloisters built by the direction of the will of John Walker, a native of the town. There are eight columns with the central

Steam train on the Settle-Carlisle railway at Kirkby Stephen

four set forward and supporting a triangular gable and a bellcote. On the inner wall is a notice announcing the terms of the Market Charter.

Kirkby Stephen Station is located to the south-west of the town, on the scenically famous Settle to Carlisle line. The railway is a tribute to the Victorian engineering skills. At one time Kirkby Stephen had two stations; the other serving the Penrith to Barnard Castle and Tebay lines.

The large sandstone parish church of St Stephen, with an impressive perpendicular tower, c.1506, dominates the northern approach to the town. It is the third structure: first a Saxon foundation, then a Norman building, c.1170, which was replaced in 1240 by the existing church. Later on, this building was much altered and enlarged to its present form. Its monuments consist of tomb chests of two famous local families, the Musgraves and the Whartons. There is the effigy of Sir Richard de Musgrave, d.1409, wearing jousting armour and another Musgrave together with his wife and sons lying in a plain tomb. The figure of Thomas, first Lord Wharton, is wearing plain armour and the tomb chest also contains the figures of his two wives. Their two daughters and two sons kneel on the sides of their tomb.

Other monuments include: a Scandinavian hog-back tomb stone and fragments of an Anglo-Danish cross shaft, with vine leaf interlace and a bearded figure. There is an elaborate pulpit of polished red and green marble, 1892.

The Walks

From the Market Place in Kirkby Stephen, pass the public toilets on the right, descend the high walled lane of Stoneshot and turn left down a flight of steps. Bear left and cross Frank's Bridge, a seventeenth century stone footbridge across the River Eden. At the far end is a boulder of Shap granite erected in memory of Geoffrey Harker, 1912-1992, by the Rotary Club of Upper Eden.

Turn right, walk along the river bank to a kissing gate, and continue by the river passing a stout stone barn to meet a footbridge. Here, the Ladthwaite Beck runs in an attractive wooded gorge. Ascend the path through the woods and continue along the track. Cross over the dismantled railway line and proceed along the green lane to meet the stream, Broad Ing Sike. Bear left and walk into Nateby to reach the B6270 Swaledale road. Turn left and walk a few paces to reach a track opening on the right with a footpath sign.

Negotiate the steps over the wall and head along the narrow walled track, with lichen-covered stones, to reach a small gate in a fence. Carry on up the track to another small gate and then across to a step stile. The way then follows a wall bordered with trees; note the skilful way in which the stones have been laid over a rock outcrop. Continue alongside a hedge-cum-fence to reach a stile leading on to the road. This gap is flanked by two large stones and a small, neatly constructed gate. Walk down the lay-by for a few paces to a gate on the left and proceed across the pasture to a gate in the corner. Follow the wall to a metal gate, pass an electricity pole, to a stone step stile in the wall. At this point there's a bit of a stretch down on the other side, in order to cross the dry (hopefully) stream bed. Make for the far bank where the wall meets the beckside. Accompany this boundary keeping straight on when the wall becomes tumbled and follow the groove beneath stunted trees to a gate in the corner.

On the far side of the beck, the farm Ridding House is derelict; its interior open to the elements, although the barns seem in good condition. Directly ahead rise the inviting grassy flanks of Green Bell. Ascend the slope on a south-east bearing to reach a point where the gradient levels out in the area of Bells; then go forward on a bearing between east-south-east and south-east. As the ground beings to rise again, aim for two slender stone pillars on the skyline – no, not the top! Whilst climbing the grassy slopes look back for fine views to Wild Boar Fell, Swarth Fell and the Howgill Fells. Proceed up through a small area of old quarry workings, passing the two slender cairns and continue to ascend until the ground levels out on the escarpment ridge. Walk to the summit cairn on High Pike Hill, 2106ft (642m).

From the cairn, initially, retrace your steps, and then descend the grassy

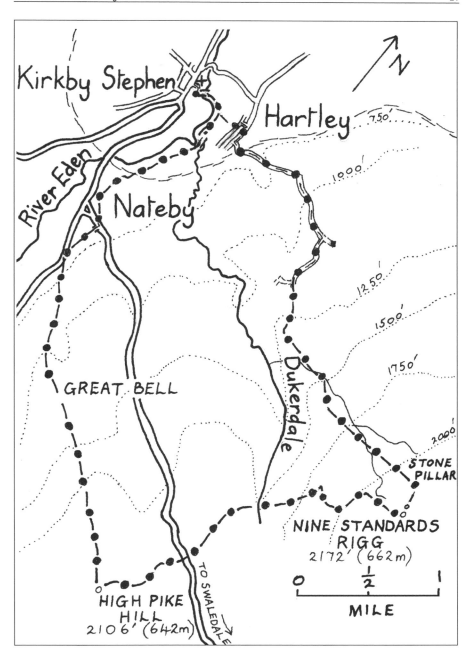

N

Kirkby Stephen

Hartley

750'

River Eden

Nateby

1000'

1250'

1500'

Dukerdale

1750'

GREAT BELL

2000'

STONE PILLAR

NINE STANDARDS RIGG
2172' (662m)

0   ½   1

MILE

HIGH PIKE
HILL
2106' (642m)

TO SWALEDALE

escarpment edge on a northerly bearing. If the visibility is clear, aim for a peaty area on this side of the Swaledale road and then bear left round the western edge of some emerging limestone to reach the road. Cross over to the BW sign indicating Rollinson Haggs and Hartley, and continue in a northerly direction across the limestone pavement. From Lamps Moss bear north-east to reach the retaining wall at the head of Dukerdale. From this point there is an impressive view down the valley of Rigg Beck; this limestone canyon is the habitat for many species of mosses and wild flowers.

The path dips to cross the stream and follows the wall passing a small ruined structure. The wall slants away as the route traverses round a grassy depression and crosses Rollinson Gill. Ascend the slope to reach another ruined building on the crest of the slope. Continue up to a finger post and admire the splendid view of the Eden Valley, the Pennines, the Howgill Fells and Wild Boar Fell. You are privileged indeed to be looking at a beautiful landscape that is second to none in the country.

From here, gradually ascend past old coal workings to reach an area of peat hags. It is preferable and easier on the ground surface to traverse on a northerly bearing and then ascend to the tall cairns on Nine Standards. These substantial stone pillars afford good protection from the wind. There are many theories attached to these dry-stone cairns: that they were set up to deceive an enemy into thinking they were the advance guard of an army, or more likely, to determine the territorial boundary between Yorkshire and Westmorland.

Walk across the top to the topograph erected by the Kirkby Stephen Fell Search and Rescue Team, 2162ft (659m); GR. NY 825 064. Walk forward to the OS column, which indicates the summit of Nine Standards Rigg, 2172ft (662m).

Retrace your steps back to the stone cairns on Nine Standards and descend in a westerly direction. The route is well-cairned, with flat stones over some peaty sections and a footbridge across a peat gully. The surface gradually improves to become a pleasant grassy way and passes a number of shake holes indicating a change in the bedrock. The route arrives at a footpath sign that indicates the Permissive Path to Nine Standards, Coast to Coast Walk, as well as a notice detailing the Green, Blue and Red Routes.

The track follows the wall as the pleasant descent enables one to sample the expansive views in a wide arc ahead. Carry on past an area of boulders and stones on the right and a small roofless building on the left. Follow the track to reach a gate and continue to descend to another gate and the fell road. Keep on the metalled surface past Hartley Quarries and descend into the village of Hartley. This is an attractive collection of houses and cottages on either side of the narrow beck that flows parallel to the road.

Hartley, Hartecla, 1285. The first element is possibly Hardres – wood; the second, cla or clea – claw: a wood near the junction of two streams. The manor of Hartley had belonged for several generations to the Harcla family, which took its name from the place, and built a stronghold on a knoll above the village. In the middle of the fourteenth century Hartley Castle became the seat of the Musgrave family. It was to become one of the finest castles in England and surrounding the building was a beautiful park well-stocked with deer. At the beginning of the eighteenth century it was recorded that the castle was nothing more than a wreck; the building having been stripped of its lead, timber and stone to enhance the other Musgrave home of Edenhall.

The site is now occupied by Hartley Castle Farm dating from medieval, eighteenth century and later times. There is now only a fragment of the medieval castle wall in the farmyard and part of the vaulted cellar to the castle kitchen.

From the village take the signposted path. Hartley Lane, between buildings, for a short walk through the meadows and along the river bank to reach Frank's Bridge. Turn right up a flight of steps, then right again and ascend the narrow lane Stoneshot. This way leads directly to the Market Place in Kirkby Stephen.

Castles of Upper Eden

Route: Dalefoot, Thringill Beck, Nateby, Wharton Hall, Lammerside Castle, Southwaite, Dalefoot

Distance: 6¼ miles (10km) circular walk

Highest Elevation: Carr House 886ft (270m)

Total ascent: 489ft (149m)

Maps: 1:25000 Explorer OL No.19; 1:50000 Landranger No. 91

How to get there: M6 junction 38, A685 to Kirkby Stephen, then B6259 via Nateby. Or, M6 junction 37, A684 Sedbergh to Moorcock Inn, then B6259 to Dalefoot.

Start/finish point: Dalefoot; grid reference NY 7790 0450

Terrain: Field paths and river valley walking

The Walk

At Dalefoot, cars may be parked on the flat grassy area close to the River Eden. Walk south down the road for a short distance to a footpath sign by the corner of the wall and on to a stile over a fence. Bear left and follow a faint grassy track which gradually becomes clearer. The route is a very pleasant terraced way across the hillside, and after an initial climb soon levels out. When the track begins to climb again, leave it, and follow the wall on the left. Energetic folks can keep to the track, ascend grassy Green Bell, and then descend to meet the route further on by Ridding House. Otherwise, keep straight on and descend bearing slightly right to reach ruined Ridding House. The farmhouse is roofless, open to the elements, but the barns seem to be in good condition.

Keep the left of the deep ghyll of Thringill Beck, and approach a gate on the left in the corner of the wall. Follow a groove beneath stunted trees, and continue past a tumbled section of wall to a gate. Head straight on keeping the wall on your left to reach the beckside. Descend to the right, cross (hopefully) the dry bed and heave up to a stone step stile over the wall. Walk to the left by an electricity pole and a solitary tree to meet a gate. Continue along the side of the wall to a gate in the far corner. Proceed across a small pasture aiming for a gate ahead leading on to the road. Turn right for a few paces up the lay-by, and take the footpath on the right. A very neat job has been done here, with a gap between two large stones covered by a small gate.

Follow the hedge-cum-fence to the left, when the boundary changes to a wall lined with trees. Look over the wall and note how the dry stone walling has been skilfully laid on the rock outcrop. Proceed to a step stile in the

Pendragon Castle

corner and bear left to a small gate. Walk down the track to a small gate in a fence, and carry on along a narrow walled way. Note the lovely bright green lichen-covered wall which is just one attraction here for water-colour artists. Climb the steps over a wall to reach the Swaledale road. Turn left and walk into the village of Nateby.

At the road junction head across to the Black Bull Inn, and proceed through the car park to a stile with a small gate. Walk part left across the limestone pasture to a stile in a fence, then on to a gate, and descend the slope to the River Eden. The river at this point is deep and dark. Turn left and proceed along the riverbank to reach the bridge.

Slant up the grassy slope in front to reach a gate leading to the environs of Wharton Hall. This ancient site now a farm, is one of Cumbria's best surviving examples of a late medieval building. The first dwelling which was erected during the fourteenth century consisted of a hall and side wings. Later, Thomas Lord Wharton erected a new Great Hall and kitchen. But it is the gatehouse that remains an impressive feature; it was originally three storeys high. Today, although roofless and without floors, it still displays the Wharton coat of arms and the date 1540. The Great Hall is no longer standing, although the back wall remains, together with the spacious kitchen and its very large fireplace.

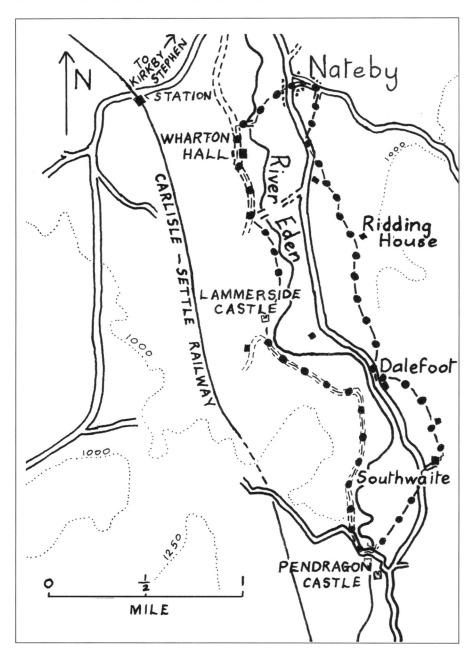

Walk past the house and outbuildings and continue down the concrete surfaced track to reach a cattle grid near to Mire Close Bridge. Do not cross over, but proceed ahead for a few paces to a gate on the left. Bear slightly left and continue across the field to reach a gate. Descend half left to a gate and carry straight on crossing a small watercourse. Ahead, the right of way leads to a small gate at the bottom of the field. Slant up the pasture to the right to meet a gate just before the tumbled remains of Lammerside Castle.

Reputed to be the home of the Whartons, the building was originally a 14th-century pele tower; it was oblong in shape, with the present remains constituting part of the central section of the fortress. The ground floor rooms were tunnel vaulted, and a corridor once ran from north to south. It is possible to note the remains of two storeys, part of the central pele tower and the extent of the thick rubble walls. The structure needs to be stabilised, and possibly given some degree of protection.

Leave the castle ruins, and head across the field descending to a gate. Turn left and pass through another gate to reach the river. Walk along the river bank and gradually climb a little with the Eden down below. The route is now grassy underfoot passing a limekiln on the right. The aspect is a very pleasant one indeed, rising ground on one side and open views across the river and the surrounding dale on the other. Ultimately, the track becomes roughly surfaced as it nears the minor road. Turn left on the bridleway sign, descend on the road over a cattle grid, and pass Low Cocklake to reach Castle Bridge over the Eden. Walk up to the road junction, and bear right to a gate for a view of Pendragon Castle.

The ruins of the castle stand on a knoll close to the banks of the river. Traditionally, it was the stronghold of Uther Pendragon, father of King Arthur. it was certainly a Late Norman pele tower built originally without any extensions. In the reign of Henry II, Pendragon belonged to Hugh de Morville, but in 1268 the estates passed equally to de Leyburne and de Clifford. The castle was kept in good repair against the border raids by the Scots, but was burnt by them in 1341, and restored by Roger de Clifford between 1360 and 1370. It was ruined again in 1541, after another attack by the Scots prior to their defeat at Solway Moss in 1542. The castle lay in a ruinous condition until 1660, when Lady Anne Clifford, Countess of Dorset and Pembroke restored the fortress. It was only after a long and bitter lawsuit that she finally inherited the Clifford estates, and set about re-roofing the Keep, building an enclosing wall, outbuildings and gates, and also constructing Castle Bridge over the Eden.

Lady Anne died in 1676, and Thomas Earl of Thanet dismantled the tower ten years later. The castle became a source of building stone, and it is more than likely that a number of dwellings in the dale contain some

Pendragon masonry. It is interesting to note that the Keep had walls 10-12ft (3.04-3.65m) thick, and that the castle entrance lay on the north side.

The castle is private property, and was sold in 1962 by one of Lady Anne Clifford's descendants, on the sale of the Appleby Castle estate. The new owner hopes to clear it of rubbish, and recently some stabilisation work has been carried out on the outer walls.

Return down the road to Castle Bridge, and use the stone step stile on the right-hand side just before the bridge. Proceed to a step stile in a short section of wall, ascend the sloping pasture keeping to the left of a roofless barn, and go on to meet a stone wall and step stile. Head forward in the same direction to another stone step stile in a short wall section, and continue across the pasture to meet a gate, a footpath sign and the road.

Turn left along the road for a short distance, and then turn right up the lane to Southwaite Farm. This name is derived from the Old Norse and means South Clearing.

Bear left to pass in front of the house, then swing right to a gate and ascend the slope. At the top slant left to a gate and into a hollow; ascend the far side to follow the wall, then walk across the pasture to dip down and cross Southwaite Gill. Climb up the opposite bank to reach a wall step stile, and go forward to stride over a small watercourse. Looking back there are good views of Dalefoot, Birkett Common and Wild Boar Fell.

The right of way leads to a gateway and a derelict farm, Carr House. Pass in front of the building, cross the stream and walk up the track as it swings up through a small wooded area. Carry on past a roofless stone structure to meet a wall stile. Beyond, for a short distance, the way is overgrown with bracken, but continue to follow the rutted track alongside the wall. Proceed round the corner to reach a step stile in a fence. Descend the grass slope to a footpath sign and onto the road at Dalefoot. Turn right and walk along to the starting point on the flat grassy area by the River Eden.

Garsdale Head and Grisedale to Cross Keys in the Rawthey Valley

Route: Garsdale Station, Rowantree, Grisedale, Whin Stone Gill, Blea
                       Gill Bridge, Uldale House, High House, Cross Keys, Cautley

Distance: 8½ miles (13.6km) linear walk

Highest Elevation: Round Ing Gill, 1,378ft (420m)

Total ascent: 489ft (149m)

Maps: 1:25000 Explorer OL No.19; 1:50000 Landranger No. 98

How to get there: By train to Garsdale Station, M6 junction 37, then A684
                       Sedbergh to Hawes Road at Garsdale Head

Starting point: Garsdale Station; grid reference SD 7884 9180

Finishing point: Cross Keys, Cautley; grid reference SD 6978 9687

Terrain: Moorland paths and tracks. No path on ground in middle
                       section

The reader may ask the question, 'Why plan linear walks?' As a fan of long distance walking in general, I rather care for the plan of following a route across an area of countryside, and finishing the day at a different location than the one I started at in the morning. There are a number of circular walks to choose from in this book to suit most walkers, but some people may have the time to enjoy a mini expedition; in that case, overnight accommodation could be considered. This walk, Garsdale to Cross Keys, Cautley, could link up with a number of crossings of the Howgill Fells.

Garsdale on the Settle to Carlisle line was the former junction with the Wensleydale railway. You may be interested to know that work has already started on the projected possible reinstatement of a passenger rail link between Garsdale and Northallerton. For further information contact the Wensleydale Railway Association; P.O. Box 159, Richmond, North Yorkshire DL10 9AA.

The lovely green upland valley of Grisedale (The Valley of the Pigs) is known to many as 'The Dale that Died'. Farming in the hills has always been a difficult business, and sadly, lack of a steady income forced many of the families out of the dale. Now there are only a small number of inhabited farms, and the others lie abandoned, ruinous and empty. Afforestation has crept into Grisedale and there is now a sizeable block on the slopes of Grisedale Pike. It would be more beneficial to the landscape generally, not just only for commercial purposes, if stands of broad-leaved trees could be

View to the Howgill Fells, Yarlside and Cautley Spout

planted in sheltered spots; they would provide a visual contrast, as well as being of benefit to birds and wild life.

The Walk

From Garsdale Station walk down the road to reach the A684. Cross over to a gap stile with small gate and footpath sign, and ascend the slope following the wall to reach a stile. Follow the path in grassy surroundings with a steep slope on the left tumbling down to Grisedale Beck. The stream has managed to cut a narrow gorge to escape from the confines of the dale to join the Clough River.

Approach a gap stile, with small gate and footpath sign, but look back for a view of Garsdale Station in the middle distance. The path wends its way through moor grass, with electricity supply poles slanting off to the right, and pass the building of Blake Mire. Facing you is a notice with the words BEWARE OF THE FARMER – lovely touch of humour here.

Pass through the gap stile in the wall and walk on ahead to cross a small watercourse. Ascend briefly to reach a gap stile and proceed past a barn to meet a wall stile and a footpath sign. Carry on, descend to cross a small stream using stone slabs and go forward to a gap stile. In front is the derelict farm of Rowantree. Ascend the meadow on a clear path keeping to the left of

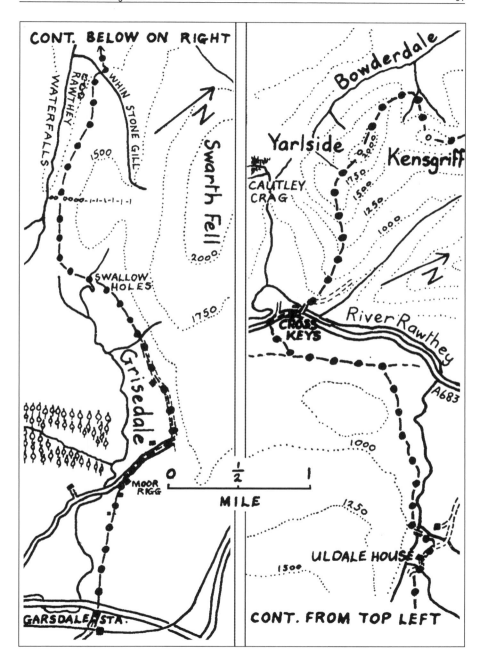

a barn to reach a gap stile, and then continue across the next pasture. Head towards the farm Moor Rigg to meet the road at a footpath sign indicating Garsdale Head. Bear right, pass the farm and walk to a gate across the road.

The narrow road changes from a metalled to a part-metalled surface as it approaches a gate in the wall. Continue to ascend to arrive at the building, East House. Beyond the house, as the little road ascends it changes to the status of a track and follows the wall to meet the open fellside. Bear left and take the grassy track alongside the wall. After a short distance on a harder surface, the way passes a barn with a few trees lining the wall, and an old limekiln standing to the right.

Cross Flust Gill by a small copse of trees to a gate on the opposite bank. Walk past a barn on the left to reach another gate, and pass into open moorland between a good stone wall on the right and a tumbled one on the left. The surrounding land is quickly being overrun by moor-grass, brown bent and sedge. Pass through a gap in a stone wall; it is sad to see more tumbled walls, and what was previously cared for pasture now returning to moorland. Continue forward to pass through a wall gap and then alongside a broken wall and a fence.

This section of the route is wet and ill-drained as you approach an unopenable gate. Climb over, cross a watercourse and proceed on to a ladder stile over a wall. Nearby, is a gate of indeterminable vintage. Continue through sedge and rush as the wall on the left descends away down the slope.

You are now standing on open moorland where there is an opportunity to gaze at the surroundings.

Grisedale is a quiet and unsung place; but for many people it is a favourite dale for moorland walking. It is flanked by the sprawling slopes of Baugh Fell on the one side, and the more inviting grassy sides of White Birks Common and Swarth Fell. All around are the sweeping moors that rise ultimately to the limestone and gritstone of Wild Boar Fell and the Upper Eden Valley.

Keep on the same heading with a faint trod on the ground. You will soon be aware of drier ground underfoot as the path passes shake holes. Keep on the lip of a depression where the skeletal ribs of limestone poke out of the ground. Follow the narrow path noting a small, round tumbled sheepfold below to the left. All about, the various shades of green mingle together on hill slopes that are gashed by dark-sided streams and watercourses. A simple pleasure, but look at the yellow, paler tints at the tips of grass, rush and sedge contrasted against the vivid greens of mosses and lichen.

Bear slightly left round an area of shake hole and protruding limestone, and pick up a faint path. Down below lies another tumbled sheepfold. There are views of dark patches of peat on the far side of the valley and a sighting of the Howgill Fells. Ahead is the entrance to Rawthey Gill, where the stream is quickly reinforced by other tributaries. Having passed the limestone area the route contours round to be parallel with the Rawthey. Keep above the river, not too high up, and continue across the moor over the watershed with no path on the ground. The surface is wet with rough tussocky grass and clumps of rush and sedge. If your direction is accurate you should meet a gate in the fellside wall.

Ahead the ground descends towards the river, so you can either bear left towards the enclosures, passing through two gates to reach a copse of trees; or, keep the height across the moor, to reach the track at Whin Stone Gill at the same point as the lower route. The lower route affords the opportunity to study the upper waterfalls on the Rawthey. This part of the valley is called Uldale.

Descend on the track to cross Whin Stone Gill Bridge and proceed to a gate. Descend the open fellside with a fine panorama of the Howgill Fells. Note the trees down by the river, bear down to the right, and cross over Blea Gill Bridge. Ascend to reach a gate, pass through a yard slant right to another gate and arrive at Uldale House.

There is an interesting fact or two about Uldale House. During the surveying of a route for the Settle to Carlisle railway, there was a possibility of the line coming through Grisedale and Uldale. As there would be a road as well, the house was built as a speculative venture for the purpose of operating as an inn. Above the door is a panel, I.S. HULL 1828.

Pass through a gate, and ascend the track with a shelter belt of trees on the right to reach another gate. Turn left through a gate and descend on the track through mixed woodland, with some fine specimens of oak, beech, birch and pine. There is a view to the right of Needle House set in lovely wooded grounds.

Pass over the refurbished footbridge and enjoy the River Rawthey cascading over a series of rock steps. The river then flows through a dark tree-girt chasm. Bear right and gradually ascend the track with more views of Needle House. From the fellside one can see the white-painted stonework, stone mullions, little dormer roofs with small stone decorations, and large chimneys on the main roof.

Continue along the track passing an old limekiln on the left. Across on the east side of the river there are green pastures, clumps of deciduous trees and plantations of conifer, compared with the rough fell on the western bank. Although a little bit wet in places, the track still continues to ascend gradually, but levels out to meet another track.

Turn left opposite to a gully with little rock outcrops and proceed on a good firm surface. This fellside route is an excellent vantage point for the Howgill Fells, which now extend along the far side of the Rawthey Valley.

When you have reached a point roughly opposite to the waterfall Cautley Spout, turn right on to a faint trackway. Descend the slope, where the route becomes faint through grass and rush, then becomes clearer to reach a gate in a stone wall. Pass a stone barn and descend to a gate. The view of the Howgills is now dominant, as the track zigzags its way down the slope to reach a gate and a footpath sign. Turn right and walk the short distance along the road to the Cross Keys at Cautley.

Across the Howgill Fells

Route:	Cross Keys, Cautley, Ben End, Yarlside, Kensgriff, Randygill Top, Green Bell, Stwarth, Ravenstonedale
Distance:	8 miles (12.8km) linear walk
Alternative (A):	Cross Keys to Sedbergh via Bowderdale Head, Hare Shaw, The Calf, Bram Rigg Top, Calders, Arant Haw, Winder, Sedbergh
Distance (A):	7 miles (11.2km)
Alternative (B):	Cross Keys to Howgill Lane via Bowderdale Head, The Calf, White Fell Head, Breaks Head, Fell Head, Beck House, Howgill Lane.
Distance (B):	6¼ miles (10km)
Highest Elevation:	Main Route: Yarlside 2096ft (639m)
Total ascent:	2762ft (842m)
Maps:	1:25000 Explorer OL No.19; 1:50000 Landranger Nos 98, 91
How to get there:	M6 junction 37, A684 Sedbergh, and then A683 Cautley; or A66 to Brough, then A683 Kirkby Stephen to Cautley
Starting point:	Cross Keys, Cautley grid reference SD 6978 9687
Finishing point:	Ravenstonedale grid reference NY 7230 0405
Terrain:	High fells, steep grassy slopes map and compass skills required.

The Walk

From the parking area above the Cross Keys, leave the road, descend the steps and cross the footbridge over the River Rawthey. Ascend the steep grassy slopes, a continuous steady ascent, with every excuse to stop and look at the views. The climb up Ben End affords fine scenes down the Rawthey Valley, the crags bordering the waterfall Cautley Spout, and east to Wild Boar Fell and Swarth Fell. It is a tedious climb, but one that is comfortable if you take it steadily. Halfway up the slope the gradient relaxes a little, and a wall comes into view in front. Beyond lies Westerdale, and behind you is a widening aspect of Uldale.

Concentrate now that you've had a breather; as the slope steepens again ahead in grassy conditions. The final section gradually eases with a faint trod appearing on the surface.

Depending on a good visibility, the short distance from the crest of Ben End to the summit of Yarlside is equivalent to payment by results:

Summit of The Calf, Howgills

First Stage: Superb Views to Stainmore and the Pennines beyond the Eden Valley; to the Mallerstang Edges; to Nine Standards Rigg; to Whernside; to Great Coum; to Ingleborough.

Second Stage: Pen-y-ghent.

Third Stage: The Lakeland Fells from Coniston to Carrock.

The grassy summit of Yarlside, 2096ft (639m), is occupied by a small cairn. All around grassy slopes are rising and falling away into the distance with many hollows and valleys. Directly ahead the sinuous course of Bowderdale Beck follows the valley of Bowderdale.

From the summit of Yarlside descend the long grassy ridge in a north-westerly direction, both flanks falling steeply away. The eastern side facing the Saddle and Little Randy Gill is steep and smooth sided, with little to get a grip on. Continue to descend the grassy ridge, to a point near to the confluence of Great Randy Gill and Little Randy Gill. Cross the little Randy Gill stream and ascend the side of Kensgriff. Halfway up there is a convenient coffin-shaped boulder for a short rest stage, and a chance to spot a number of fell ponies usually in the vicinity. Continue the climb to reach the neat cairn on the summit of Kensgriff, 1883ft (574m).

Walk along the ridge in a north-easterly direction and descend gently to

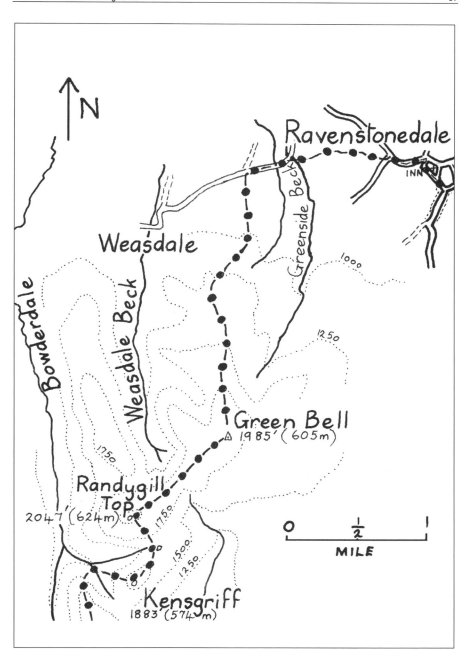

reach a small peaty pool. Climb the grassy slope ahead on a north-westerly bearing, to arrive at the cairn marking the rounded summit of Randygill Top, 2047ft (624m). Follow a clear path in a north-easterly direction to descend the slope towards Stockless. Given a good day, there are many rewards for being on the Howgill Fells. Again, there are expansive scenes across to the Mallerstang and Wild Boar Fell, down the Eden Valley to Cross Fell and to Ingleborough and Whernside. There's a marvellous canvas of cloud-dappled slopes that are coloured green, brown and burnished gold.

At the col, Spengill Head, note the steep slopes to the left dropping down to the valley of Weasdale. Proceed on a clear trackway amongst a paradise of rounded hills and steep-sided valleys. Ahead lies the Survey Column, OS 10805, marking the summit of Green Bell, 1985ft (605m).

From the summit walk on a northerly bearing on what appears to be a tractor route. The going is easy with pleasant grassy conditions underfoot. On reaching the plateau of Stwarth, continue to head on a northerly bearing, but keep an eye out for a wall coming in a little way on your left. Gradually turn on a north-easterly heading and descend across a number of grooves and tractor tracks; but keeping on the higher ground between Pinksey Gill and Poskey Bottom. What splendid names!

In the lower fellside stages, there are wet patches to dodge, but aim for a manure collection point, grass is greener here for obvious reasons; and if your navigation is perfect, you will arrive at a solitary boulder by the farm road.

Turn right along the road for a short distance, and turn right through a gate at a bend. Go forward to another gate, cross the bridge over the stream and along a track towards a barn. Continue up the track hollow to reach a gate in the wall. Carry on across the field towards the corner of a wall and a newly planted tree area. Follow the way between the wall and the fence to reach a gate, and continue ahead alongside a wall through the field to meet another gate. Keep straight on down the grassy way, a BW between walls to a gate, and from here pass through two more gates to reach the road.

Turn left down to the road junction, then turn right and walk over the bridge to the King's Head Hotel. Turn right passing in front of the Hotel, and follow the back road into the centre of the village of Ravenstonedale.

Section 2: The Westmorland Plateau

Stretching away to the east from the Lake District fells is an area of limestone country, the Westmorland plateau. This upland terrain is bounded on the west by the River Lowther, with the River Lune to the south and the River Eden to the east and north.

Walking on limestone is a joy; the sheep cropped turf blending in beautifully with the crinkled, naturally sculptured surface of mountain limestone. There is great pleasure in hearing the rock 'tinkle' underfoot, and noticing the little pools of rainwater trapped in the surface hollows. There is ample opportunity to study the great variety of limestone flora; indeed, the tiny cracks and crevices support many tiny ferns, mosses and flowers. However, in wet weather care is needed as the limestone surface becomes slippery underfoot.

An area like Asby Scar is one of the best-developed and least damaged examples of limestone pavement in Britain. The whole surface area is covered with an impressive mass of contorted rock in the form of crinkled scars, ledges and terraces; a veritable moonscape that has to be seen to be appreciated.

Asby Scar is under the care of English Nature; in the past, other areas of nature's rock garden have been ravaged by individuals and commercial interests who have taken the stone for domestic gardens. Thankfully, there are now severe restrictions concerning the extraction of this unique rock formation.

This limestone plateau has been the home for prehistoric inhabitants, and after many years of fieldwalking by local archaeologists, they were able to shed some light on the origins and living practices of these early peoples.

The fort of Verterae became an important, strategically placed station for the Romans. A garrison some five hundred strong, guarded their main supply road to the north. It commanded the country on the route between York and Carlisle.

The importance of the route over Stainmore also became evident to the Normans, who took over the site of the Roman fort and constructed a powerful castle. Although attacked and largely destroyed by the Scots, the fortress rose from the ashes to become a dominant influence at the head of the broadening Eden Valley.

In the sixteenth century it was repaired by that great northern benefactress, Lady Anne Clifford. Later it became neglected to become a source of ready masonry. Much of its fine stone was removed to supply the extensions to Appleby Castle.

Many quiet, attractive villages are to be found situated in wooded hollows amongst the limestone uplands. They lie on the banks of crystal-clear streams that flow out of the limestone. There are fine old houses to see and a wealth of ancient churches; one with an interesting rushbearing ceremony.

Although much of the lower land is enclosed as small fields, the higher ground is largely open fell country. This is another fine area of walking country, that is well supplied with a network of paths and tracks just waiting to be explored.

A Walk in Limestone Country –
Crosby Garrett and Potts Valley

Route:	Crosby Garrett, Smardale Bridge, Brownber, Potts Valley, Potts, Crosby Garrett
Distance:	9 miles (14.4km) circular walk
Highest Elevation:	Ewefell Mire 1,004ft (306m)
Total ascent:	640ft (195m)
Maps:	1:25000 Explorer OL Nos.19, 2; 1:50000 Landranger No. 91
How to get there:	M6 junction 38, A685 to Kirkby Stephen, then side-road via Soulby. Or, A66 to Brough, then A685 to Kirkby Stephen and side-road via Soulby
Start/finish point:	Crosby Garrett grid reference NY 7280 0940
Terrain:	Limestone uplands, pastures and valleys

The name Crosby Garrett is derived from Old Scandinavian Krossabyr, a 'by' with crosses. Garrett is derived from a French personal name, Gerard. In 1206 it was known as Crossebi Gerard. Note: The familiar place-name ending '-by' is from byr, the Old Scandinavian work for village or settlement.

This quiet village approached along hedged lanes lies at the end of by-roads, and set in a fold in the surrounding limestone upland. The farms, houses and cottages stand on either side of Crosby Garrett Beck, and over-looking this pleasant rural scene is the church standing on a hill at the north end of the village. A number of footpaths, tracks and bridleways focus on the village, and it is surprising that the Settle to Carlisle railway does not have an unmanned halt here for the benefit of visitors and local residents alike. The station was closed in 1952, and surely, it is time for a re-assessment of trans-port requirements for Crosby Garrett, as it is at the hub of a superb walking area. The village is ideally placed to explore the lovely limestone uplands and the charming valleys of Potts Beck, Scandal Beck and upper Lyvennet Beck; together with a number of interesting villages and hamlets.

St Andrew's Church stands in a commanding position offering splendid panoramic views across the surrounding countryside. There is a lovely aspect over the Eden Valley to the distant Pennine Hills.

This is an interesting old church, with the remains of a very early arch, probably Anglo Saxon, above the fifteenth century chancel arch. The north arcade was built by the Normans, with large round pillars, and the capitals decorated with carved leaves and heads. The original church was widened

Crosby Garrett

and given a north aisle in about 1175. On the western side of the building there is a projecting bell turret, probably of the thirteenth century.

The Walk

Walk to the south end of the village on the road and pass under the railway viaduct. Beyond the cattle grid the way becomes a roughly surfaced track. At a fork, take the left-hand track and ascend alongside the wall, having negotiated beds of nettles. Approach a stone step on the left and continue up to another stile in the wall. Aim for the end of a wall across the field and go forward to a gate. Proceed across the meadow to a stile in the wall, continue to a gate, which was fastened up, and on across the field to a gap in the wall. Carry on to the next wall gap, aim to the left of the wall end in front, and head on that bearing across the field. On reaching the wall, there is a crumbling stile to climb over, and made all the more difficult with loose stones. Go over the pasture to a wall step stile and bear slightly left to follow the boundary wall.

Look over on to Smardalegill Viaduct and the lovely leafy valley of Scandal Beck.

In the days of the London North Eastern Railway, L.N.E.R., this remote valley once had its own railway station. Also of note, is the splendid

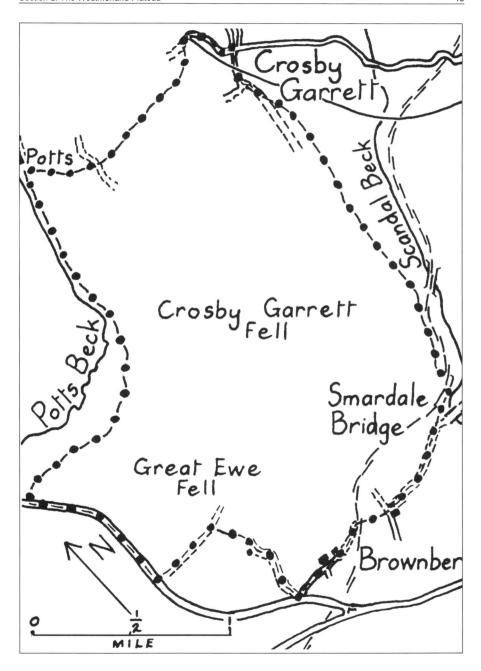

Smardalegill Viaduct, which gradually became unsafe after the closure of the line. It is to the great credit of all organisations and bodies concerned that the viaduct was saved from collapsing into the valley; it was saved for posterity as a tremendous feat of engineering skill. Smardale is now in the care of the Cumbria Naturalists Trust, and it would be courteous to seek permission before entering the Reserve.

Walk across the sweet limestone turf to a wall stile above a derelict building. At this point there is a notice for Coast to Coast walkers. This is not our route, but refers to the line of the long distance route in the immediate vicinity. To avoid damage to the archaeological site please follow the waymarked permissive path alongside the boundary wall.

The archaeological site in question is the Severals Village Settlement, which was passed through on the original Coast to Coast route. The area was a complex of prehistoric settlements with important evidence of field boundaries, hut foundations, dykes and sunken ways

Continue on through a gate and cross the bridge over the old railway track down to meet a track. Turn left if you wish to view Smardale Bridge, otherwise, bear right up the track and carry on to a gate. Proceed to another gate and follow the track between walls. Pass through a gate at Friars Bottom Farm, turn left, then go right through a makeshift gate and along a narrow way between walls. Approach a gate, cross the course of the old railway and continue down the track to reach a farm complex at Brownber. Keep straight on down the farm road for a short distance, and walk ahead down the track passing through a small copse of trees to a cattle grid.

Turn right immediately, through a gate, and follow the pleasant leafy way. There's a wall on one side and a border of trees and thorn bushes on the other. Pass a stone barn and go through a gate into a meadow. Walk to the right of the building called Intake to meet a gate. Then slant left up the pasture. Look back for superb views to the Howgill Fells, Wild Boar Fell, the Mallerstang and Nine Standards Rigg.

Approach a gate in the wall and bear left along a fairly clear track. Looking to the north-north-east there is a sighting of the cairn on Great Ewe Fell. Continue to follow the boundary wall until the fell road is reached. Turn right and walk to a cattle grid where a notice announces: BENTS FARM, CAMPING BARN; Tel: 015396 23681

The surrounding countryside is particularly lovely: rolling smooth hills, undulations, dry valleys, the white 'bones' of limestone peeping through the surface, stone walls, isolated farms, lone trees or small clumps of ash and above all a discernible lightness that is the quality of a limestone landscape.

A faint track leads off to the right past a small quarry – not a right of way. Descend on the road towards Fell Head and take the next track on the right. The track leads directly towards copses of trees, a barn and boundary walls.

Ahead, the lovely Potts Valley begins to assume a definite inviting form. Amongst grassy surroundings the track descends between scree, outcrops and limestone scars, with a patch of woodland just ahead.

Potts Beck is a beautiful, crystal clear stream flowing over a limestone bed; sheep and humans can count themselves very fortunate to be in such a place. On the right is the impressive Hazzler Brow Scar towering above the grassy slopes. This is truly a secret valley that shyly and slowly reveals its charms. However, it does allow a sneak peep at the distant Pennine hills.

Walk alongside the wall with the beck on the other side; and then it's along the beckside with the wall on the other bank. You are now in an area where the grass looks so inviting that it is a great temptation to enjoy forty winks. Approach a step stile on the water's edge, and then forward to a stile in the wall by a gate. Continue to a derelict farm ahead, walk to a gate, but don't go through it towards the building. Potts Farm has not been lived in for forty years; and it seems such a shame that a building that has been a home for generations, and so full of character structurally, is being allowed to crumble and decay.

Turn right up the slope alongside a wall as far as the corner. Then turn left, and continue to follow the wall up the slope to a wall stile just above a gate. Proceed up to a gate and another wall stile. Carry on ahead with a stone barn in the field to the right. Go through a gate, cross a track, and walk through another gate in front to the left of a wall. Passing a solitary gatepost is the clue for an expansive view of the Eden Valley, Nine Standards Rigg and the Mallerstang.

Proceed through a gate and enter a walled grassy track Ladle Lane. Bear a little to the left, then to the right and keep straight on along a section which is a little damp underfoot. Further along there are beds of nettles, long grasses and numerous wild flowers. As the track widens better progress is made to meet another track coming in from the left. Cross the bridge over the Settle to Carlisle railway line, and walk down the road into the village of Crosby Garrett.

Maulds Meaburn and Wickerslack

Route:	Maulds Meaburn, Lyvennet Beck, Crosby Ravensworth, Slack Randy, Dalebanks Beck, Wickerslack, Maulds Meaburn.
Distance:	7.5 miles (12km) circular walk.
Highest Elevation:	Ewe Locks 978ft (298m).
Total ascent:	617ft (188m).
Maps:	1:25000 Explorer OL No. 19; 1:50000 Landranger No. 91
How to get there:	M6 , junction 38, B6260 to Orton and Maulds Meaburn Moor, then side road to Maulds Meaburn village. Or, A66 Appleby, B6260 and side road to Maulds Meaburn.
Start/Finish Point:	Maulds Meaburn, grid reference: NY 625 162
Terrain:	Gentle limestone countryside, pasture land and the wooded valley of the Lyvennet.

The second element of the place-name Maulds Meaburn is derived from the Old English maed 'meadow', and Maulds is derived from Maud, who was married to William de Veteriponte.

The village lies in the valley of the gently meandering Lyvennet; that flows from its source amongst the bare limestone upland, to richer pastures and woods on a bedrock of sandstone.

The Walk

From the village green cross the bridge on the road leading to Maulds Meaburn Moor, and take the lane on the right signposted Crosby Ravensworth. Meet a cattle grid between gates with a stone wall on the right. Approach a stone gateway surmounted by beasts' heads; the entrance to Flass House – the name means, 'the house by the river pool'.

Go through the small gateway on the left marked public footpath. Follow the wall, with a good view of the house, and continue past a barn on the left; then under a stone bridge and into a meadow. Squeeze through a stone stile, cross a stone slab, and walk along the river bank to a footbridge over a water course. The stepped squeeze stile in the wall is a beautiful specimen – should be given the accolade of the finest stile in Westmorland.

Proceed along the wooded river bank, with some fine trees, to a small gate in a wall. Continue by a stone-built house, Low Row, to meet the road. Note the attractive arched bridge over the Lyvennet Beck with its resident colony of ducks. Bear left along the lane past the farm, with weird shapes of Westmorland limestone on the wall. Swing round to the right, and then slant

Maulds Meaburn

right, down to a footbridge and a stile on the left. Continue along the river bank noting the tower of the parish church of St. Laurence. This fine building in Crosby Ravensworth, beautifully situated amongst trees, is of great architectural interest. Dating from 1190, the crossing is the oldest part, but with centuries of alteration and extension, the church has many fascinating and interesting features.

The path proceeds along the river bank to meet a step stile in a fence. Cross a small pasture to another stile, and walk towards a tall ladder stile on the right. Head left, and exit via a gate. Go forward to a ladder stile on the right, and bear left along the fence, with trees and bushes, to a step stile in a fence. Circumnavigate a large fallen tree – it is a bit early in the morning for obstacle courses! Walk alongside the fence passing scattered glacial boulders of Shap Granite – note the elongated crystals of feldspar. Approach a step stile in the fence and bear right across the pasture. Then incline left towards the river bank to reach a stile in the corner, and on to the road at Holme Bridge.

Turn right, and walk to a road junction. Bear left and proceed on a metalled surface – although there is a pleasant grass verge. The track, called Slack Randy, ascends gently, and the metalled surface soon ends, with lovely soft turf alongside the track. Keep to the right where the track forks, with the stone wall still on the right. Pass a pile of huge Shap boulders and the remains of an old limekiln in the wall.

You are now completely on grass, so keep following the wall. Pass a single glacial erratic, as the wall bends to the right. There are more boulders here in the angle of the wall, and also a brief appearance of a limestone pavement. Beyond the confines of the stone wall, are the remains of the extensive British settlement – a complex group of hut foundations and walled enclosures called Ewe Close.

Keep on straight ahead as the wall bends away, with the buildings of Lane Head in front. Go through the gate by a sycamore tree to the right of the farm. Proceed down a narrow grass paddock to reach some ruinous barns on the right. Go through a gate on the right, and then swing left down the field towards a lone ash tree. Continue down the depression in the slope to reach Dalebanks Beck.

There is a small patch of tree cover by the stream, so head for the left-hand edge to cross the water course. Bear right along the grass track to High Dalebanks. On the opposite side of the track, approach a gate, and head to the left up the slope, with the WM indicating Haberwain Lane and Crosby Ravensworth. Follow the wall to a stone step stile. Incline left up the slope to reach a gap stile in the far corner of the wall. Note the wall foundation of large Shap boulders, and follow the wall to a gate. Beyond, the stile is blocked, so pass in front of the farm of Haber and then swing left round the buildings. Go through the wall gap stile in front and into the field.

Ascend the slope diagonally to the right towards a wall corner, where there is a way over into the next field. Follow the wall on the far side up to a gate at the top, and then aim for the top left-hand corner of the next field. Continue ahead through a narrow paddock, turning left at the top. Go through a gate to pass High Haberwain Farm and on to meet Harberwain Lane. Turn right and walk to the end of the wood, and then turn left on to a grass track. Proceed through a gate and along the edge of the wood, through a gap in the wall, and continue on the grassy way. Could this be an old coaching route to the hamlet of Wickerslack? At a point where the track bends, go through a gap stile ahead into a small pasture. Walk down to a gate in the wall and bear right. Continue through the complex of farm buildings at Wickerslack. Go through a gate into a walled farm track. Where the track bends, proceed straight ahead through a gate, and walk alongside a wall to meet another gate.

The scenery changes, with conifer plantations ahead. Follow the fence and descend the slope of a large pasture to the end of the wood. Turn right, and go through the small gate. The route appears to be blocked in front, but bear to the right past the farm buildings to reach a gate in the fence. In

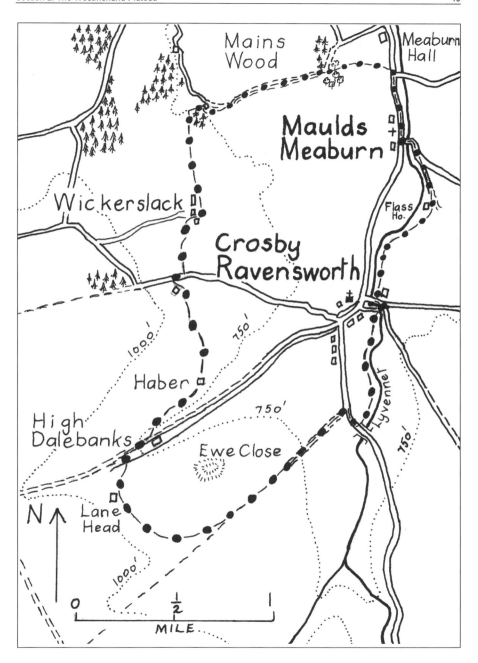

summer time, there may be some vegetation growth to negotiate along this section.

Go through the gate and follow the clear track ahead, which descends to a gate in park-like surroundings. Continue to a second gate, and on to a third gate to enter Mains Wood. At a point where the track bends, head straight on at a WM, and follow the path as it descends to a step stile. Enter the large pasture and cross Howe Brook by means of a small bridge. The way then slants right towards a wall stile with a WM to reach the road. Away to the left along the road, stands Meaburn Hall, a stately house built in 1610.

Turn right, and walk down the road into Maulds Meaburn, back to the starting point.

Great Asby & Gaythorne Plain

Route:	Great Asby, Dale Beck, Gaythorne Hall, Gaythorne Plain, Great Asby Scar, Sayle Lane, Great Asby
Distance:	8½ miles (13.6km) circular walk
Highest Elevation:	Gaythorne Plain 1,230ft (375m)
Total ascent:	823ft (251m)
Maps:	1:25000 Explorer OL No.19; 1:50000 Landranger no. 91
How to get there:	M6, junction 38, B6260 to Orton and Bank Moor, then side road to Great Asby. Or, A66 Appleby, B6260 and side road to Great Asby
Start/finish point:	Great Asby grid reference NY 6800 1318
Terrain:	Limestone moorland and limestone scars

The place-name Asby is derived from Askabyr, a 'by' (Old Scandinavian for village) where ash trees grew. In 1160 it was known as Aschaby. This is an attractive village set in a shallow wooded valley. The houses, cottages and its Green lie on both sides of Asby Gill, and are connected by a road bridge and footbridges. Now a peaceful farming community, Great Asby is surrounded by smooth upland slopes underlain by limestone. To the south of the village the landscape changes to a higher rugged area of outcropping limestone. This is known as Great Asby Scar and forms one of the best examples of limestone pavement in Britain.

Great Asby is part of an area of limestone country bounded on the west by the River Lowther, with the River Lune to the south and the River Eden to the west and north. South of Appleby the ground is generally higher, and in the main, lies between 650ft (198m) and 980ft (229m), reaching a height of 1352ft (412m) at the southern edge of Orton Scar. Although much of the land is enclosed as small fields, the higher ground above 880ft (268m) is largely open fell country used mainly for sheep grazing.

The village has a number of things to interest the visitor. As well as a variety of pleasing, warm-coloured, stone-built homes facing the beck, there is Asby Hall, now a farmhouse. This old building was built as a mansion for the Musgrave family, and a panel above the door bears the heraldic arms of the Musgraves, the initials E.M. and the date 1694. The church rectory hides a secret, because its north wing is actually an ancient fourteenth century pele tower which was reconstructed in the seventeenth century. Another interesting fact is that the Rectory has one of Lady Anne Clifford's notable door locks, which is similar to the one in Dacre Church. The example at Great Asby is initialled A.P. and dated 1670.

Close to Asby Gill is the location of St Helen's Well, which is a consistent and powerful spring of pure water. Helen was the mother of the Emperor Constantine.

There is thought to have been a church here in Norman times. The present church of St Peter, constructed in 1866, stands on the Green; it is a simple, high-roofed building with a spacious interior. Inside it has an attractive east window depicting scenes in the life of St Peter, and note the carving of musicians supporting the roof beams. As you walk to the south end of the village look for the tiny seventeenth century stone footbridge over Dale Beck.

The Walk

From the south end of Great Asby, turn right at the footpath sign indicating Scale Beck, Highfield and Gaythorne Hall. Continue along the metalled surface, cross over a cattle grid and the beck to pass a scar on the left. Carry on past a barn and over another cattle grid as the farm road begins to climb the slope. The hard surface is a little tedious to walk on, but you can comfortably use the pleasant grass verges.

Take the right-hand fork when the lane bifurcates and continue to ascend the hill. There are now good open views to be enjoyed across the Asby Valley. Eventually, cross a cattle grid and proceed straight on to reach a stile by a gate, when the farm road turns right for Halligill Farm. Follow the wall on the right to a step stile with WM, and slant to the right down a pasture passing a number of erratics of Shap Granite. Cross the stream to a gap stile in the wall ahead. It is now open country with limestone walls; note the rapidly deepening course of Halligill Beck to the right with its enclosure of trees.

Proceed up the rough grass pasture ahead, still bearing slightly right close to a small copse of trees. Look for the step stile in front with a WM. From here, slant down the pasture slope to reach a step stile and a gate. Cross a small stream, and continue in the same direction when Gaythorne Hall comes into view. Pass a WM on a short post and down to a gate, then along the track to the right of this lovely house.

This grey-stone building, probably Jacobean, is remotely situated in the upper valley of Scale Beck. It consists of an interesting square design with a projection on each wall, these being occupied by two staircase wings and two porches. The house displays the shield of the Bellingham family, but has been a farmhouse for many years.

Bear left at a finger post indicating Gaythorne Cottages, and proceed in front of the house to a small gated paddock. Continue straight ahead along

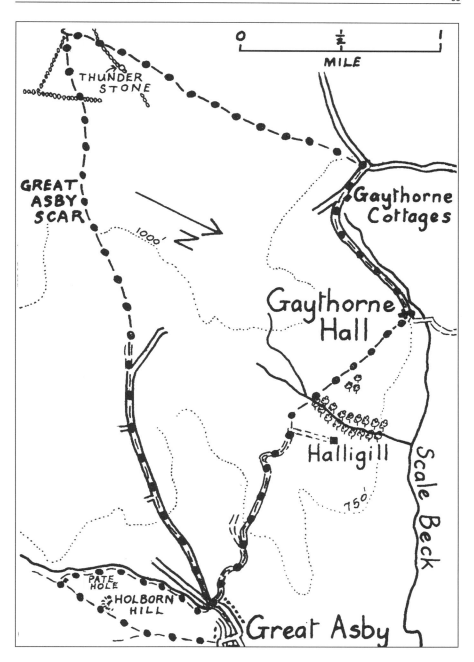

the metalled farm drive, with the advantage of soft grassy verges. Cross over a cattle grid and ascend the slope to reach Gaythorne Cottages. Bear right and note the brave stand of wind-blasted trees. Proceed up to the road junction and strike off left, due south, across Gaythorne Plain. There is no indication of a path on the ground, and the conditions underfoot vary from rough tussocky grass, fine grass and the uneven surface of a limestone pavement. Walking on this southerly bearing will lead you to the right of an uneven circular area confined by a stone wall. Pass a quarrying site to meet one of the main boundary walls running across the plain. If you desperately wish to visit the Thunder Stone, and you have religiously followed the course of the route, you will need to bear left for a short distance. The said object is situated at a bend in the main wall south of the quarry. It consists of a large glacial erratic of Shap granite that is basically part of the wall, and most likely, serves the purpose of a Boundary Stone.

The surrounding limestone uplands have been recognised as the home of our distant ancestors. Many prehistoric habitation sites have been discovered, such as: settlements, enclosures, stone banks, sunken ways and isolated burial cairns. Some of the main sites are indicated on the OS 2½ inch map. Over many years of fieldwalking, archaeologists have discovered a wealth of small flint artefacts: unworked flints, scrapers, cores, flint and chert blades, grit tempered pot sherds, microliths and arrow heads, dating back to Mesolithic and Neolithic times.

Keep your eyes skinned when you are passing areas of soil disturbance caused by rabbits and moles. On many occasions these creatures have brought up to the surface numerous and varied flint artefacts.

Continue alongside the boundary wall to reach a gate. Clearly visible on the rising ground ahead is the monument on Orton Scar. The stone cross was raised to commemorate the Jubilee of Queen Victoria in 1887, by the loyal subjects of Crosby Ravensworth.

Step over the loose concrete blocks that constitute a stile and descend the slope. Ahead, the view is of a marvellously rugged limestone landscape of scars and pavements leading to the summit of Castle Folds. Look for the stubborn solitary tree on the escarpment skyline. Aim for a gate at the bottom, but just before reaching the opening, cut back to the left, and walk diagonally away from the lower wall. Continue across the grass to meet a step stile in the side wall. A notice announces: ENGLISH NATURE – WELCOME TO ASBY SCAR.

Aim for the grassy depression ahead and walk on a terrace between the limestone pavements. Keep bearing slightly right after a quarry track is sighted on the left. Walk towards a depression in front under a small scar – recognisable as a small V-shaped gap through the limestone terraces. Descend a grassy groove and then through bracken with a wall coming in

Beacon Hill to the Howgill Fells

from the right. Accompany the wall to a step stile, or if you miss it there's a gate further on. There is an explanatory notice by the gate.

The information goes on to explain that Asby Scar is one of the best developed and least damaged examples of limestone pavement in Britain. In geological terms, the limestone was laid down when the area was a shallow, warm sea. After millions of years, earth movements caused the limestone to be forced upwards, and the surface pavement was created by glacial action.

Visitors are warned to take great care in wet weather when the limestone surface becomes very slippery.

Slant down towards a gate and continue along a grassy track to another gate. Follow the walled track to meet the minor road. From this point it is a straightforward walk along Sayle Lane back to the village of Great Asby.

Great Asby: short circular

Route:	Great Asby, Holborn Hill, Asby Gill, Town Head, Great Asby
Distance:	2 miles (3.2km) circular walk, can be combined with previous walk. See sketch map on page 53.
Highest Elevation:	Holborn Hill 755ft (230m)
Total ascent:	164ft (50m)
Maps:	1:25000 Explorer OL No.19; 1:50000 Landranger No.91
How to get there:	As for Great Asby and Gaythorne walk
Start/finish point:	Great Asby; grid reference NY 6800 1318
Terrain:	Field paths and alongside Asby Gill

The Walk

From the centre of Great Asby cross the road bridge over the beck and walk up the track ahead signposted Little Asby. On reaching a gate continue up the grassy way between walls. The route then widens into a long thin pasture with a grassy grooved track on the left-hand side. Approach a small gate with a WM and continue between hedges to reach another small gate with a WM. Proceed straight on past a wall gap, and go forward through a gate ahead on a tractor track to a waymarker post. Follow the blue arrow alongside a wall towards a gate. Bear slightly right across the pasture to a gate. Here, there is a marker post with a blue arrow. You now enter a large irregularly shaped field, the site of an ancient settlement.

The site of Holborn Hill consists of a stone bank enclosing a roughly oval area. Inside this area are further grass-grown banks, forming interior sections. It possibly dates back to the Iron Age or native Roman times.

Walk down the sloping pasture to a gate and carry on to another gate, each with blue waymarkers. Proceed across a small thin pasture to a gate and follow the wall to reach a stone barn. At this point, turn right beyond the barn keeping on top of the slope, and not following the wall into the dip. Continue along the grassy edge to meet a wall corner ahead. Note the WM placed on a scrubby thorn tree, and walk alongside the wall to reach a simple step stile over a fence. Carry on along the fence to another step stile, and descend the track to a meadow beneath the sloping valley side.

From here walk in the direction of a gap beyond, and pass a fine example of a limekiln on the right. Bear left through a gap towards an area of limestone pavement and the stream side – a charming and most delightful spot. Note the cave under the scar on the right.

This is called Pate Hole, and with few limestone caves in the area, is

Great Asby: stone footbridge

ranked as the largest. A low entrance leads to a passage with pools, the flood channel, and beyond, progress is only possible for a limited distance.

Walk ahead and pass through a gate into a large meadow, and if you go and have a look at the stream you will discover that it has done a vanishing act. Proceed along the stream bank over limestone pavements, and with outcropping scars of limestone on both sides of the little gorge. It's pleasant underfoot too, with close-cropped turf to walk on. Continue through a gate and follow the fence noting that the stream bed is still dry, even in winter. Keep to the left of a track rising to the right, and follow the WM to a step stile over the wall in the corner. Bear left, cross the gill, and walk up to the road junction with a children's play area nearby. Turn right and stroll down the road to the starting point.

Brough and Great Musgrave:
fine rivers and an ancient castle

Route: Brough, Sowerby Park, River Belah, Daleholme Lane, River
                        Eden, Scandal Beck, Great Musgrave, Hall Garth, Church
                        Brough, Brough

Distance: 10¼ miles (16.4km) circular walk

Highest Elevation: Verteris Hill 627ft (191m)

Total ascent: 371ft (113m)

Maps: 1:25000 Explorer OL No.19; 1:50000 Landranger No. 91.

How to get there: From M6, junction 38, then A685 via Kirkby Stephen, or
                        junction 37 via Sedbergh, or Penrith to Scotch Corner A66

Start/finish point: Brough grid reference NY 7955 1458

Terrain: Field paths and riverside ways

The place-name Brough usually refers to ancient camps, usually Roman ones. In 1198 it was known as Burc, in 1228 as Burgh and in 1279 as Burch inder Steymor.

The town of Brough consists of two parts, Church Brough and Market Brough and is collectively called Brough-under-Stainmore. Modern road improvements to the A685 and the A66 have now bypassed the respective settlements of Church Brough and Market Brough.

The route across Stainmore, the Stony Moor, was known by people of the Bronze Age. This trans-Pennine route was most likely improved by the Romans, who built their fort at Brough (Verterae) to guard their strategically important main supply route north from York to Carlisle. Situated on a small rise on the north bank of Swindale Beck, its design was of the normal rectangular 'playing card' shape, with the longer axis running north to south. The fort was further strengthened by the construction of defensive ditches and was probably manned by a garrison of five hundred soldiers.

After the departure of the Romans from these islands the site was taken over by Britons for their own defence. On the arrival of the Normans, it is not surprising that part of the Roman fort was used as the site for the building of one of the earliest castles in the north of England. The castle was started about 1095, but was largely destroyed by the Scots in 1172. It was rebuilt in 1174 to serve the same important purpose of controlling the Eden Valley and the route over Stainmore.

As part of Hugh de Morville's estate, the castle was forfeited to the Crown soon after the murder of Becket in 1170. It remained the property of the Crown until 1204, when it was given by King John to Robert de Vipont. Eventually it passed, through marriage, into the Clifford family. In 1521, a disastrous fire gutted the interior and the building was eventually repaired by the doughty Lady Anne Clifford, Countess of Pembroke. Later, it eventually became uncared for and neglected; and by the mid-eighteenth century, much of its fine stonework had been removed to repair Appleby Castle.

Today, the moats are still well-preserved; there are some surviving parts of the original masonry, such as the great keep, the bailey walls and the fine rounded tower called Clifford's Tower. The ruins still attract one's attention, particularly when lit by the late afternoon sun.

The site is now under the care of English Heritage and is open to the public during normal hours.

The Walk

Go east past the main road junction in the centre of Market Brough and cross the bridge. Turn right opposite Dial House, and walk down the small lane alongside Swindale Beck. Turn left, and then bear left again after a house and proceed along the back lane that lies parallel to the A66 trunk road. Turn right at the end and pass through the tunnel. Turn sharp left at the other end to a ladder stile and footpath sign. Pass by the side of the farm building to reach another ladder stile. Aim diagonally across the field noting the gaunt ruins of Brough Castle to the right. There may be a little uncertainty here as the field boundary has changed but keep fairly left to reach a stile and a footbridge across the stream.

Turn right, walk along the stream side to a fence, but keep to the left-hand side of it to meet a gate. Head straight on to follow a line of thorns to arrive at a footbridge over a sike, and to a nettle-wreathed step stile over a fence. Walk forward up the slope, bearing slightly left, to reach a stone step stile in the wall.

Turn left along Leacett Lane for a little way to a footpath sign on the right to Low Park. Note there is no proper stile and the way ahead is badly overgrown. Having taken a breather looking at the view up the Eden Valley, it's time to 'gird up your loins'. The immediate need is for machetes, flails, walking sticks or even a pet goat to clear a passage. Nevertheless, you will probably have to retire defeated to the comparative comfort of the adjacent field after a few minutes of desperate endeavours. At the top bear slightly left and discover a step stile completely submerged in vegetation – Mungo Park had nothing on the intrepid souls who have battled away through this jungle. Go forth for another session of path clearing and emerge at a sort of gate. Negotiate the barrier, follow the hedge to a real gate and continue along the hedge-

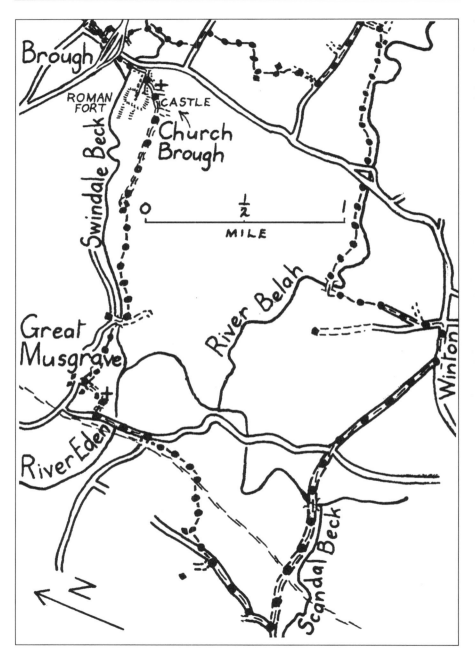

row to reach a step stile. Don't cross over, but spare a minute to admire the very fine example of a barn that is almost fortified in appearance.

Turn left down to a gap in the hedge and make for the farm Sowerby Park. Go through a gap in the fence and on to a stile in the wall corner, which has been whitened for clarity. Incline to the right down a farm track and continue along it to meet the road. Turn left and follow the road to reach a boulder at the entrance to a farm drive. This splendid glacial erratic of Shap granite has the name of the farm, Hollins View, carved into its pink surface. What an imaginative idea!

Proceed a little further on and turn right at a finger post. Walk down the hedge track and bear right through a gate at a point where the track bends. Descend to another superb barn, sadly, roofless and ruinous, but still bearing a magnificent doorway and fine red-sandstone quoins.

Walk along the bank of the River Belah to pass a boundary stone with a cryptic 9 on its surface. As the river bends go straight on ahead across the meadow to a gate beyond. Continue along the grassy way in a lovely mini-valley midst leafy surroundings; whilst the river flows over flat bedrock into dark, deep pools. Proceed along the river bank to a gate and go forward to a simple, but ergonomically correct stile. The river is now tree-fringed, making this section an enjoyable riverside walk. As you approach a step stile in a wall, note the gorgeous colour of the impressive sandstone Belah Scar on the far bank of the river. Ahead, there's a gap stile in the wall by the old Belah Bridge.

Turn right for a few paces to a footpath sign and a step stile on the left and walk across a small pasture to a step stile in the hedge. Cross the busy main road to the opposite verge to a footpath sign and continue along the river bank to a stile over a fence. Walk straight ahead across a large field to reach a farm bridge over the Belah. On the far side turn left, slant up to the right to a gate, and follow the fence to a second gate. Further on beyond another gate, the route now continues as a track between hedges. Turn right on reaching the main road, noting that the village of Winton, with a convenient hostelry, is situated just a short distance away.

Keep on the grass verge for a little way and turn right along Daleholm Lane which, although metalled, is quiet and peaceful with grassy banks, wild flowers, shady trees and verdant hedgerows. Walk straight across the B6259 road and carry on along a trackway between hedges. To the left there is the fine aspect of Beckfoot House gazing out across the fields. Just prior to the Eden and its confluence with Scandal Beck, there is a plot of land planted with trees by Cumbria County Council to commemorate the Queen's Jubilee Year, 1977. The long footbridge spanning the River Eden is a splendid spot for lunch; here you will be able to enjoy a tranquil scene of green meadows and calm waters.

Continue along the grassy hedged track following Scandal Beck. The track widens and passes through the course of the old L.N.E.R railway, from Barnard Castle to Penrith, to meet a by-road to Soulby. Turn right and proceed along another quiet lane to pass the entrance to Low Hall. Take the path just beyond on the right indicated by a gate and footpath sign. Follow the fence round in front of the house called Smithfield and go forward to a gate. Looking back there are good views to Wild Boar Fell, Nine Standards Rigg and the hills beyond Brough.

The route follows the fence lined with trees and bushes to pass beneath the former railway line. The gate is intricately fastened with barbed wire and cannot be opened. Bear left and pass over a couple of step stiles alongside the old railway track bed to reach a stile and footpath sign. Turn right and, at the road junction bear left, then walk along the B6259 for a short distance to Musgrave Bridge. On the far side of the bridge a path leads to St Theobald's Church. [See the separate account of Great Musgrave, its church and rushbearing ceremony, pages 64-66.]

From the gate bear left and climb up Church Lane into the village of Great Musgrave. Looking across the green and beyond the line of scattered dwellings, rise the exciting forms of escarpments, summits and plunging slopes of the Pennine hills.

Turn right and proceed up to some gates, then take the path immediately on the left to a gap stile in a short section of wall. Continue straight on across a small field to a gap in the hedge to appreciate a fine panorama of the surrounding hills. Head for the right-hand side of the farm, Hall Garth, towards a gate and the road. Turn right, then right again down the track and pass over the bridge across Swindale Beck. At a footpath sign bear left through a gate. Walk through the beckside meadows and keep straight on past another footpath sign. Go round the left-hand corner of a fence to a hurdle; then across the field with a fence on the left and aim slightly right towards a clump of trees at the foot of rising ground. The line of the route is uncertain here and it would be helpful to have waymarkers along this particular section. There is a step stile over a fence, but ahead the right of way was submerged by a mass of growing crops during the last reconnaissance of the route. The footpath had been ploughed under and the closely growing crops made progress extremely difficult (this obstruction has been reported to Cumbria County Council).

Pass through the small metal gate at the far side of the field; then continue along the hedgerow passing a small barn, and reach a gate at the beginning of a hedged track. There are no problems now and you are soon rewarded with a good view of Brough Castle. Proceed down to a gate and stile, then bear left on a track showing signs of a cobbled surface as it climbs through a sandstone cutting. This is a good example of a once important ancient trackway leading from the castle. One can imagine the passage of knights on horse-back, fine ladies, soldiers, servants and villagers many centuries ago.

The church of St Michael, which is situated to the right, is a long, low structure of Norman foundation, c.1150. Evidence of its Norman features are to be seen in the masonry on its south side, especially the south doorway. West of this entrance is a Norman window, and inside the church there is the tower arch and the north arcade. The splendid three-storeyed tower dates from the years 1513-1525, and the rest of the building dates from the four-teenth century to the early sixteenth century. The nave has a splendid oak roof and there are some fine eighteenth-century brass memorial plaques.

The ancient trackway leads to The Square in the heart of Church Brough. This is a pretty, rectangular area lined by stone-built houses which includes medieval Church Hill. At the far end of The Square there is a triangular green complete with a sycamore tree and a maypole, on the site of the original market cross. During the coaching era the centre of the village once contained two inns.

Turn left at the end of The Square and walk down the road to cross the bridge. Aim half right to a footpath sign and follow a trackway leading to a rickety step stile. Continue along a grassy path to reach a ladder stile and emerge onto the main road. Bear left, pass under the A66 and cross the road to the path alongside Swindale Beck. Follow the stream back to the starting point in the centre of Market Brough.

Great Musgrave: a short guide

3 miles (4.8km) north of Kirkby Stephen, lies the quiet, peaceful village of Great Musgrave. This is one of the villages in Cumbria which still observes the colourful and ancient custom of rush-bearing. The church set on the river bank below the village can be seen from the road bridge over the River Eden. The track bed of the former Penrith to Barnard Castle railway lies deserted, bridge gone, station gone. The railway was a casualty of the P.M.C.R.L. – the Popular Movement for the Closure of Rural Lines. Its crime, the railway had ceased to pay its way! The route over Stainmore was one of the finest scenic journeys in the land. Memories are crystal clear of the expansive views down the Eden Valley from high on the hillside slopes beyond Kirkby Stephen; the magnificent viaduct over the River Belah, and the high and lonely Barras Station, a welcome and much-loved port of call at the end of a good day's walking in Swaledale. There is nothing quite so sad as a departed railway. The rejuvenated Settle to Carlisle line crosses the western extremity of the parish, and for some considerable time, volunteers, friends and supporters backed by County and Parish Councils, fought hard and ultimately triumphed to preserve this magnificent route through the northern hills. Many a departed railway would have given their last sleeper, chair and rail to have had such dedicated support. A similar movement is now flourishing to restore the Wensleydale Railway from Redmire to Garsdale Head.

St Theobald's Church, Great Musgrave is a very thin building with a slim and elegant tower. It sits neatly against rising ground alongside an ancient track up to the village. An impressive avenue of horse chestnut trees leads to the church across a pleasant riverside meadow. Two former churches have already slid into the river and, in 1883, floodwater entered to a depth of over 4ft (1.2m). The River Eden is justly famed for its trout and its grayling and it was over the churchyard wall in 1880 that the first grayling

Great Musgrave church

were tipped as fry. The fine stony bed suited the fish and they have multiplied and established themselves. The Eden here is placid and flows gently past soft banks decked in velvety turf and bordered by tees. This idyllic stretch of the river is much beloved by anglers.

The rush-bearing event is held annually on the first Saturday of July. About twenty-three churches in England observe such a rite. Of these, five (Ambleside, Grasmere, Great Urswick, Musgrave and Warcop) are in Cumbria. The ceremony dates back to the fourteen century, and was the formal re-laying of the rushes which covered the earth floor of the churches in former times. Change in use over the years and the appearance of stone floors in churches allowed the ceremony to become more akin to May Day celebrations, with young girls carrying crowns of flowers. The custom of the boys' rush crosses dates from the 1930s.

The ceremony in its present form has been observed for at least fifty years. The celebrations commence with a gathering outside the Village Hall. Led by a local silver band, the procession of children bearing floral crowns and rush crosses and accompanied by clergy and parents, walk through the village and down the road to the church. The final part of the route is along the track through Green Garth beneath the lovely canopy of trees to the church door. Inside the building the floral garlands and rush crosses are placed by the altar. Verse 1 of the Rushbearing Hymn is as follows:

Rush-bearing procession

On this our holiday
We wear these crowns of flowers
Now bringing to thy table Lord
These floral gifts of ours

A mid-nineteenth century account of the rush-bearing ceremony states, "The rushbearers are led up the north aisle of the church and they hang up their garlands on the side – there to remain until the next year. The gospel is read by the clergyman, some prayers are offered and psalms sung. Afterwards, the clerk and the vicar retire, a space is cleared near the altar, a fiddle is produced and dancing continues until three or four o'clock in the afternoon".

After the present-day service, the gathering walks up the old sunken lane to the village and the celebrations are concluded with tea, buns, crisps, pop and sports. Finally, a collection is taken outside the Parish Institute and divided amongst those who carried crowns and rushes.

Section 3: Appleby and the Eden Valley

As you enter the town it is clearly noticeable that the roadside sign states, Appleby-in-Westmorland. The inhabitants wished to preserve a link with its former status as a county town. Boroughgate is a handsome thoroughfare lined with trees and verges and flanked by a number of interesting buildings. At the top of this splendid street is the High Cross bearing the famous inscription: RETAIN YOUR LOYALTY, PRESERVE YOUR RIGHTS. Just below is Lady Anne's Hospital, an almshouse founded by Lady Anne Clifford.

At the foot of Boroughgate is the Low Cross, and the entrance to the lovely old church of St Lawrence. The lower part of the street contains the ancient sixteenth-century Moot Hall, and also the present-day market area.

Appleby Castle is situated on a hill, surrounded on three sides by the River Eden which loops round in a complete semi-circle. The site was occupied by an earlier castle of the motte and bailey type with deep defensive earthworks. Soon after it was walled in stone, and other features such as domestic ranges were added later.

Askham on the banks of the Lowther near to Penrith, has long been regarded as the prettiest village in the district. Its wide grass verges splashed with wild flowers, form a lovely foreground to a range of houses and cottages of the seventeenth and eighteenth centuries. Askham Hall is the ancient manor house of the Lowther Estates since the dismantling of Lowther Castle. Viewed from across the parkland, the castle presents a skyline of turreted and embattled shapes.

The village lies close to the fells, and is at the end of a superb high level trek across the High Street range. From here, long distance walkers on The Ravenber route set out for Dufton across the Eden Valley, and climb the Pennines to the River South Tyne.

Close by Penrith is the peaceful village of Dacre, complete with castle and its churchyard bears.

The Eden Valley, with its villages, hamlets and farmsteads served by lanes and tracks across rich farmland, is in great contrast to the high fells and dark crags of Lakeland. The settlements are an integral part of this green, agricultural landscape. These include Morland, Kings Meaburn, Bolton and Long Marton; lovely places, each one with something of interest.

East of Penrith the River Eden follows a course regarded by many as its most beautiful stretch. This majestic river, long famous for its salmon fishing, runs through impressive sandstone gorges amongst fine wooded scen-

Almshouses, Appleby

ery. A walk certainly to savour, it traces an idyllic verdant route from the
village of Armathwaite to Wetheral.

On the east bank of the river, the land slowly rises towards the distant
fells. Here, an undulating landscape is patched with woodland and coursed
by swift-flowing streams. A secluded village hides an ancient bastle house; a
quiet footpath leads to the nettle-covered moat and ivy-wreathed tower of a
tumbled castle; a lonely track carries one to an open pasture dotted with a
wide circle of enigmatic stones; and fitting perfectly into this lovely countryside scene is a memorial birdbath to a well-loved broadcaster.

Appleby: riverside and pastureland paths to a fine waterfall

Route:	Appleby, River Eden, Great Ormside, Ormside Mill, Heights, Catharine Holme, Rutter Force, Hoff Beck, Hoff, Bandley Bridge, Appleby
Distance:	9 miles (14.4km) circular walk
Highest Elevation:	Heights 689ft (210m)
Total ascent:	410ft (125m)
Maps:	1:25000 Explorer OL No.19; 1:50000 Landranger No. 91.
How to get there:	M6 junction 38, then B6260 to Appleby. Or, A66 Penrith to Scotch Corner Road
Start/finish point:	South end of Appleby, grid reference NY 6860 1972
Terrain:	Riverside routes, fieldpaths through pastures and farmland

The place-name Appleby contains the Old English æppel which may have replaced the earlier Scandinavian work epli. It means Apple Tree village ('by') or farmstead. In 1130 it was known as Aplebi.

The town is properly called Appleby-in-Westmorland in order to preserve its link with its former position as a country town. Throughout its history the settlement has seen the coming and goings of Danes, Celts, Anglo-Saxons and Normans. It is not clear whether the Romans were active here, but their camps and roads were nearby, so it is quite possible that the site now occupied by Appleby Castle was well-known to them.

The town is situated on both banks of the River Eden which divided the settlement into two parts, the old which is the area around Bongate, and the new on the rising ground up to the castle, which is known as Boroughgate. The River Eden, therefore, flows through the heart of the town.

The new town part is famous for a wide thoroughfare descending from the castle gates to the cloisters of St Lawrence's Church. This attractive street is lined with trees and verges, and flanked by interesting buildings dating from the Georgian Period to the nineteenth century. The upper part of this splendid avenue is noted for the column called High Cross, a seventeenth century structure bearing the inscription: RETAIN YOUR LOYALTY, PRESERVE YOUR RIGHTS. Also in the upper part is the building that Lady Anne Clifford, Countess of Pembroke, founded as an almshouse in 1651.

At the lower end of Boroughgate is the ancient Moot Hall, c.1596, now the market area, and both sides of the street occupied by shops and offices; it is also the site of the Low Cross, a copy of the upper column and erected in the eighteenth century.

Appleby Castle sits on a hill and is surrounded on three sides by the River Eden which loops round the town in a semi-circle. The earliest structure, which may have been Roman, is definitely a Norman castle of the motte and bailey type built by Ranulph de Meschines. In the twelfth century it was re-constructed in stone, and the formidable Keep surrounded by impressive earthworks, was a very secure fortress. The curtain walling is largely of the twelfth century, as well as the Postern in the middle of the east range that still retains its portcullis groove. The east range which was the domestic part of the castle, was rebuilt as a stately piece of seventeenth century architecture by the Earl of Thanet in 1686-8. The work was accomplished mainly by using stone from Brougham and Brough castles.

The castle belonged to the Viponts before it went to the Cliffords in the thirteenth century, and remained in their possession until the death of Lady Anne Clifford. The castle then passed to John Tufton, the Earl of Thanet, Lady Anne's son-in-law.

St Lawrence's Church at the foot of Boroughgate is externally a perpendicular church [this is an historical division of English gothic architecture covering the period from c.1335-50 to c.1530]. The perpendicular character of the church is to be seen in the upper part of the tower and in the clerestory with its three-light windows. The lower part of the west tower contains Norman masonry, as well as the window shape in the north wall and the porch entrance on the south side. The north chapel is believed to be part of Lady Anne Clifford's family chapel, built in 1654-5. She also restored the chancel in the church.

The main monuments consist of a fourteenth century, praying effigy, the vaulted tomb of Lady Anne Clifford and the rather fine recumbent alabaster figure of her mother, Margaret Countess of Cumberland. Behind stands a panel containing an impressive family tree of twenty-four colourful heraldic shields.

Another item of interest is the nationally important organ which came as a gift from Carlisle Cathedral in 1684.

Appleby is famous, or in the eyes of some of its inhabitants infamous, for its annual Horse Fair, which is held on Fair Hill just outside the town. Large gatherings of gypsies in caravans, lorries and chromium-plated limousines gather to tell fortunes, sell goods, and buy and sell horses. Interested onlookers can watch the horses being washed and scrubbed in the Eden.

The Walk

The starting point is from a little lane that descends to the River Eden at the southern end of the castle grounds. Approach a kissing gate and footpath sign to Ormside. Go alongside a high wall on a narrow pathway to reach a step stile. Carry on into the field by the river to a step stile, and continue along the tree-lined route to a ladder stile. Pass through a small copse to arrive at a footbridge (a metal girder) and a step stile. Follow the field round to the left-hand corner to a step stile. Pass through the wood along the river bank and cross a stream to a step stile. On the map the immediate area is called Castle Scua. Proceed through a leafy area, then a wooded section, to climb a stepped bank to a WM. Bear left. You are now high above the river. Approach a step stile as the path heads to the right above Jeremy Gill; a delightful way, rich in many species of wild flowers.

On reaching a step stile over a fence, go alongside the fence to the left and descend to a footbridge. There are rock outcrops here to the right of the path. Cross over Jeremy Gill, slant right and ascend the bank. Note the narrow gorge on the right of the path, as you come to a gate and step stile. Cross over a plank footbridge and walk by the hedgerow to reach a marker arrow. Turn left through a gap in the hedge, and progress along a wide grassy pathway between hedges. Approach a gate and ladder stile, pass under the Settle to Carlisle railway, a lovely sandstone arched bridge, and continue down the track. There are waymarkers pointing straight ahead, and at a bend carry on through a gate. Proceed through the meadow to a step stile, bear left to a stile in the wall with a PF sign, and on to the road at Great Ormside.

Of considerable interest is the village church of St James which lies a quarter of a mile away to the left. Standing on a knoll above the Eden, the church is a rugged stone barn-like structure built for defence. It has a low west tower, a nave, chancel and three medieval bells, and stands on the site of an earlier Norman building. Most of the fabric dates from the eleventh century with many Saxon and Norman characteristics.

In 1823, a magnificent Anglo-Saxon highly ornamented metal bowl was unearthed in the churchyard, which also contained Viking burials. This lovely seventh-century gold and silver masterpiece may be seen in York Museum.

The area is believed to have been a Viking settlement and that Orm was their leader. Hence the village name; Ormside, Ormesheved 1256, Orm's hill.

From the footpath sign turn right to pass a farm with a well-tended lawn. The building carries a date stone, namely, 16IMG83. Proceed up to the road junction to a telephone box, turn left, and then right along a minor road. Just before Ormside Mill a clear running stream accompanies the road in a leafy, peaceful spot. There's a footpath sign at the bend in the road, so proceed straight ahead and follow the stream, Helm Beck, through the field. Walk towards a gate, pass two boulders, one of granite one of limestone, and bear half right through a small area of woodland. Cross the stream to reach a stile

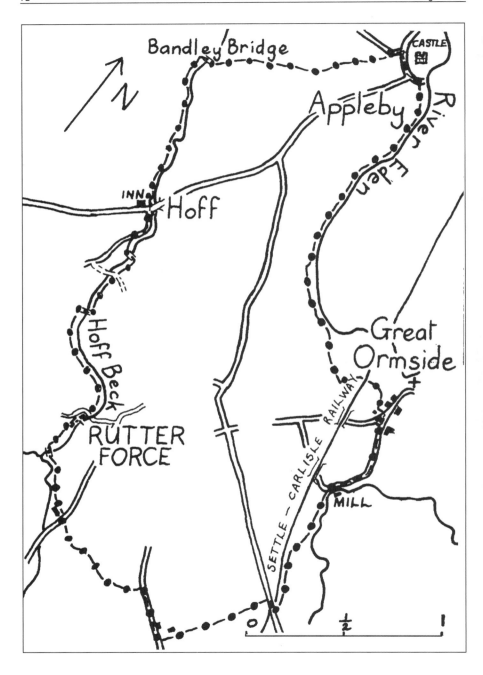

in the fence, then aim diagonally across the field. Stride over a streamlet to a stile over the fence and continue to follow the fence alongside the railway. The route climbs gently up the field to reach a footpath sign and the road. Cross over the railway bridge for a few paces and take the path on the left, with a footpath sign indicating Heights.

Walk up the field alongside the hedge to a gate. Continue straight ahead to reach gates, take the right-hand one, and carry on to a gate gap in the wall. From here proceed through the field to a gate and stone step stile, Brow Farm is now in sight. Pass through a gate, past the front of the farm, and continue down the farm track with a former quarrying area to the right.

On reaching the road turn right, and walk down the slope to a BW sign on the left indicating Catharine Holme. Go through a gate passing a small plantation, and swing round to follow the wall to a small gate. Continue alongside the wall to meet a footbridge with a lifting pole at the far end. The route follows fences, bears right to a footbridge and a gate, and proceeds left alongside trees towards a gate straight ahead. Walk down the track with farm buildings ahead to reach a gate and a BW sign. Turn right for a few paces, and then bear left past farm buildings to a gate in front. Turn left alongside the fence and go forward half left to a gate. Bear left, and then walk with a line of mature trees on your right on a lovely grassy terrace above the stream. Pass by granite boulders in the field to reach the bridge over Asby Beck.

There's a step stile ahead on the right over a fence. Walk through the meadow to a gate, at which point you are close to the beck. Continue to a step stile, and go on ahead to a small gate leading to a lane down to Rutter Force. A footpath sign indicates a route to Haybanks Cottage.

This is a good spot to linger; a knot of waterside buildings, ducks dabbling, a footbridge and a cottage providing refreshments. Rutter Force is an attractive waterfall at a point where the Hoff Beck drops some 30ft (9m) over a rock ledge. Its name is probably derived from the Old English hrutere, meaning the roarer.

A word of warning: a certain author, who shall be nameless, attempted to take a photograph of the falls from a different angle. No sooner had his feet touched the unknown, but very slimy surface of the causeway, than he achieved a perfect half base-over-apex somersault. He was last seen lying in the water keeping his camera dry with an outstretched arm.

Go through the gate on the west bank of the beck, signposted PF to Hoff, and forward to a step stile. Proceed down the pleasant riverside meadows to a stile and footbridge over Hoff Beck. The way continues along the river bank passing over a number of step stiles before reaching a farm track bridge over the beck. Carry straight on to another step stile, go forward to cross over a footbridge and walk along the track to meet the road. Turn right for the short distance to Hoff and the New Inn.

Rutter Force, Hoff Beck

Cross the main road and take the signposted track to Colby. Keep to the right and up the lane to a gate with a WM. Bear right through the gate and proceed alongside the beck to a step stile. There is now another pleasant riverside path passing through three more stiles and with the valley gradually narrowing. In front there's a clump of trees on the left and the ground rising beyond the beck on the right. You are now approaching a spot named on the map as Cuddling Hole.

Continue across the meadow to meet a step stile, bear left slightly rising above the beck to a stile, with a mini gorge down below to the right. Go forward to another stile and descend the short distance to Bandley Bridge. Cross over this rather superior and substantial footbridge to reach a metal ladder stile over a wall. Climb up the slope past a ruined building on the right and carry on to a step stile in a fence. Aim half right across the field, and scale the fence by means of a metal ladder stile, noting the large granite boulder. Turn left and pass through a gap in the hedge with a view of the Keep of Appleby Castle in front.

Approach a stile with waymarkers, and bear right along the track for a short distance to reach a gate and a metal ladder stile on the left. Follow the hedgerow ahead noting the housing estate just in front. Descend to a metal ladder stile, turn right along the track for a few paces, then bear left at a step stile. Accompany a fence and then a hedge on the right to reach a ladder stile. Go past the houses and on to a metalled surface to meet a footpath sign. Turn right along the road to the Green, and turn right again along the main road. On reaching a sharp bend descend the lane ahead back to the starting point.

A circular walk from Appleby via Dufton by quiet ways and woodlands

Route:	Appleby Station, Stank Lane, Flakebridge Wood, Greenhow, Dufton, Brampton, Appleby Station
Distance:	8 miles (12.8km) circular walk
Highest Elevation:	Castle Hill 722ft (220m)
Total ascent:	620ft (189m)
Maps:	1:25000 Explorer OL No.19; 1:50000 Landranger No. 91
How to get there:	M6 junction 38, then B6260 to Appleby. Or A66, Penrith to Scotch Corner Road
Start/finish point:	Appleby Station grid reference NY 6865 2065
Terrain:	Field and woodland paths and tracks

The Walk

From Appleby Station go down the road and turn right under the railway bridge. Continue up the road over the level crossing of the other Appleby railway line. Although dismantled, there are whispers that a Preservation Society is interested in resurrecting a section of the old line.

Proceed straight ahead to a ladder stile and a footpath sign to Hungriggs. Whilst contemplating the imminent dash across the helter skelter of the A66, it's a joy to think of the comfort and relaxation of travelling by train. Descend the steps and cross to the footpath access in the central reservation, and then another gallop across the other carriageway. Ascend the steps to the minor road and straight ahead to a ladder stile in the hedge. From the footpath sign carry on to a kissing gate and footpath sign to meet a farm road. Turn right, pass through a gate and take the hedged track on the left called Stank Lane. I doubt it was so called because people deposited their rubbish here, but more likely to be derived from Old Norse, *stong*, a pole, meaning a boundary mark.

Approach a step stile and proceed along the right-hand side of a hedge. Go on for a few paces, then slant to the right to a step stile in the bottom corner of the fence. Walk alongside the hedge to a step stile in the fence and enter a small wood. Follow the fence down the slope to a gap stile in a wall. Continue along a grass embankment and bear left on a faint track. There's a very pleasant aspect all round; a wooded slope to the west, the Pennine slopes in the distance and a green valley to walk along. Although probably a

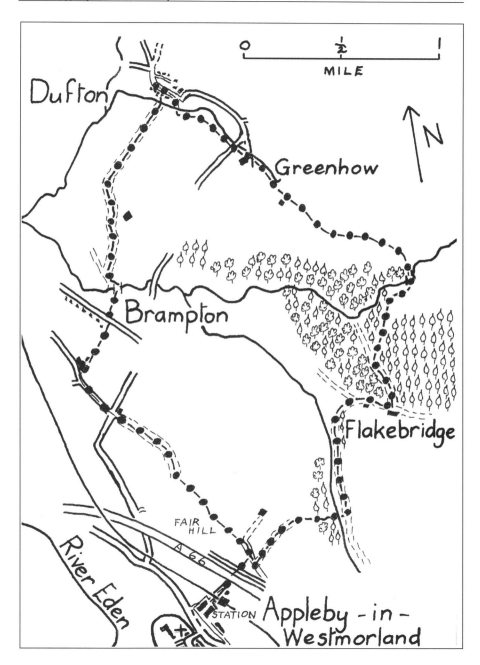

glacial melt-water channel; this hidden enclosed valley is the ideal location as a landing strip in some stirring tale about smuggling or political intrigue.

Looking ahead, there's a plantation, mainly conifer with an edging of broadleaf trees. The track follows the woodland edge to reach a gate in a stone wall. Continue over the small stone bridge, with the secret valley surrounded by wooded slopes stretching away to the north-west. Slant to the right to a gate and step stile with a footpath sign indicating three routes. Bear right, WM's on large oak tree, and continue on the track past a house of rough stone, a green slate roof, painted window mouldings and stone chimneys; the house is set low down against rising ground and overhung with trees. Walk on the direction of Flakebridge House, but turn left on a track into the woodland to reach a gate and step stile.

Climb gently through a pleasant wooded area with views of Middle Tongue Hill, the southern flank of High Cup Gill. On reaching a footpath sign, indicating Keisley, bear right, and keep straight ahead at a point where the track swings to the right. Proceed through a cleared area, cross a gully spanned by a plank and continue to reach a ladder stile over a wall. Slant up the grassy slope to a stile in a wall; it's a step up and over metal bars job. Note the very fine specimen of a sycamore tree standing close by.

Continue straight ahead through the pasture, climbing gradually to meet a step stile and a WM. Now you are rewarded with a splendid view of the neighbouring Pennine hills; from Dufton Pike, High Cup, Middle Tongue, Scordale to Roman Fell. Walk down the field, along the edge of the wood, then descend left to a stile in a stone wall and a footbridge over Keisley Beck. Bear to the right round the foot of rising ground topped by a copse of trees, and follow a red sandstone wall; a fine example of the wallers' art. Walk up the pasture passing an uprooted birch tree, and pass through the remains of a tumbled field boundary. Now bear left towards some trees by a wall and proceed to a stile. From here, follow the wall and reach a step stile in the fence. Continue along the wall to a through stile, and carry on to a gate and step stile. Pass two mature oak trees, then a handsome stone barn with a slated roof and wide doorway. The white-painted farm of Greenhow is now clearly visible in front.

Aim for a gate in the bottom right-hand wall and head for the east side of the farm buildings. Follow a fence lined with trees and bushes to meet a gate in a wall. Carry on along the track to a gate, and cross the farmyard to another gate which leads to the farm lane. Pass through a wall gap stile into the field and go forward to reach another wall stile and the minor road. Turn left for a short distance, and then take the footpath on the right signposted Ghyll and Dufton. A small gate leads to a path that accompanies the beck through a delightful leafy glade. There are old quarry faces to the left as you approach a step stile with a Woodland Trust notice – VISITORS ARE WELCOME TO WALK IN OUR WOODS.

Enter a section of the little gorge with old quarry faces on either side, as the path ascends and passes a sweet chestnut tree with fine twisted ridges on its trunk. The path descends in leafy surroundings to arrive at a footbridge. Cross over the bridge, ascend the track to meet a gate and step stile, and walk past a small car park and toilet block into the village of Dufton.

Pennine Way explorers are very glad when they arrive here after the trek from Teesdale. Some years ago, on a foul day of incessant rain, I remember fording Grain Beck at Birkdale, no footbridge then, and carrying across two youngsters who were standing rather apprehensively on the banks of the swollen stream. At the end of that day Dufton appeared as a very welcoming place indeed.

Earlier visits to the area meant a comfortable stay at the Post Office kept by Mrs Lightburn. Now, although the present establishment doesn't provide accommodation, it does have an excellent supply of chocolates, sweets, biscuits, fruit and ice-cream.

Walk past the Youth Hostel turn left, footpath signposted to Brampton, and descend on a track down to the Ghyll. Cross the footbridge and continue straight ahead to ascend the far slope through the trees. Go across a track and carry on to reach a gate and step stile. Proceed down a walled track which becomes a grassy way lined with bushes and trees. The way continues to descend gently to pass barns before bending to the left.

The track, now called Wood Lane on the map, is bordered by wild roses, sloes, crab apples and hawthorns. Still grassy underfoot, the track passes a farm to the left, bends again to reach a broken gate and climbs gradually. The route then descends to meet a footpath, bends left and keeps left through the trees to meet a footbridge. Cross over the beck, turn right and take several paces to locate a metal step stile lurking in the hedge. Prior to the footbridge, you could go straight on, cross over the stepping stones and turn left to the stile.

Ascend and follow the field boundary of bushes and trees, but remember to look back for an expansive view of the Pennine hills. Walk towards a through stile in a stone wall on the outskirts of Brampton village. Bear left for a short distance to a footpath sign on the right indicating Croft Ends. Just beyond is another stile in a stone wall with a well-executed large notice BEWARE OF THE BULL. Carry on up the field to reach a fence and buildings, where a WM points to the left. Follow the fence to a gate. Here you will find a copy of the previous warning sign. I just wonder if the size and quality of these warning notices are perhaps a wee bit intimidatory.

Bear left down the drive to reach a gate and a PF sign. Turn left along the road to reach a junction.

Proceed straight across through the gate at Clickham Farm to meet a small metal gate at the end of the garden. Continue along the grassy track, Lime Lane, to reach a step stile in a fence. Carry on ahead down the broad, hedged track to a step stile and gate. The grassy way leads to a galvanised step stile, and then continues along the field hedge with no sign of a path on the ground. There is also a small watercourse in the nearby ditch. Better progress can be made by moving higher up the slope in order to reach the stile in the fence ahead. Slant up to the right to a gate in the top far corner in the field.

The route continues to a gate and step stile, then on to another gate. Now cross over to the other side of the hedge to meet a gate, stile and footpath sign. Walk along the farm lane to a kissing gate on the right with a footpath sign.

You are now almost back to the beginning. Proceed across the field, the minor road and the A66, and then down the road back to the starting point at Appleby Station.

NOTE: This route to Dufton could be a variation of the linear walk from Askham via Dufton to Garrigill. See pages 95-101 and pages 106-112 and pages 155-164.

Glassonby:
a bastle, a castle, caves and a stone circle

Route: Glassonby, Glassonbybeck, Old Parks, Romany Memorial,
                            Kirkoswald, Eden Bridge, Daleraven Bridge, River Eden,
                            Lacy's Caves, Little Salkeld, Long Meg And Her Daughters,
                            Addingham Church, Glassonby.

Distance: 8½ miles (13.6km) circular walk

Highest Elevation: Claydubs 591ft (180m)

Total ascent: 377ft (115m)

Maps: 1:25000 Explorer OL No.5; :50000 Landranger Nos 86, 90, 91.

How to get there: leave Penrith (M6). Take A686 to Langwathby, then side road
                            to Little Salkeld and Glassonby.

Start/finish point: Glassonby grid reference NY 5765 3890

Terrain: Fieldpaths, pastures, river bank and woodland ways.

The place-name Glassonby is derived from 'Glassan's by', – Glassan's homestead. Glassan is an Irish personal name. In 1177 it was known as
Glassanebi, and Glassanesby in 1230

The houses of this small rural village are a mixture of red sandstone and
rendered walls; peacefully grouped round a triangle of land at the road junction. Here, large maple trees are a joy to behold when clothed in their
magnificent autumn colours.

White House Farm has the date 1723 on the door. There is a view of the
prominent skyline of the Pennine escarpment from the small lawn. Across
the courtyard is an interesting structure of red sandstone which could be
mistaken for just another ordinary farm building. Its lichen-covered walls
still cast a vigilant eye northwards as they have done so for many years – it is
a bastle house.

After the Battle of Flodden in 1513, the Border country was not a safe
place to dwell unless adequate precautions were taken. Bands of raiders, the
mosstroopers, made their sorties through the quiet ways in the hills to terror-
ise the scattered farmsteads and larger houses in the lonely valleys. They
came to settle old scores, to steal horses, cattle and sheep and to burn down
dwellings and crops. As the isolated communities had no hope of immediate
assistance, the inhabitants took refuge in small defensible buildings which
included pele towers and bastle houses. These structures would not stop an
army but, they proved quite formidable to a small band of raiders looking for

easy pickings and anxious to avoid determined resistance. With a few excep-
tions they are the only farmhouses in the British Isles which accommodated
livestock on the ground floor and the farmer and his family on the upper
floor.

The Glassonby bastle, which is early seventeenth century, is constructed
of large rough blocks of sandstone with ashlar dressings. The original
ground floor doorway is chamfered and rebated and has a hole for a drawbar.
Access to the strongly constructed doorway to the upper floor is by means of
an outside flight of steps set against the west wall. In the early days, the resi-
dential part was probably reached by a ladder from the lower chamber,
which could then be drawn up for safety.

Generally, the upper floor of a bastle had either timber beams supported
on rough corbelling or carried on a beautifully constructed stone barrel
vault. The end wall away from the doorway usually contained a fireplace.
The bastle roof at White House Farm is now low-pitched, but the original
kneelers remain and indicate that the roof was once steeply pitched and high
enough to have contained an attic. The bastle, which lies on private ground,
can be seen from the roadside.

The Walk

Leave by the Glassonbybeck road, and then turn left by the footpath sign
along the metalled farm lane to Old Parks. Go through the farmyard and turn
left past the house towards the left-hand gate. Carry on through another gate
into the field beyond. Over to the left, set on a grassy hillock, is a small railed
enclosure containing a sandstone birdbath on a pedestal. For closer inspection, it would be courteous to ask the farmer for permission to view. This
memorial commemorates a much-loved children's radio naturalist. The
inscription on the plaque states:

"Sacred to the memory of Revd. G. B. Evans, Romany of the BBC. Whose
ashes are scattered here. Born 1884. Died 20th November 1943. He loved
birds and trees and flowers and the wind on the heath."

*[Publisher's note: Romany enthusiasts may wish to note that Sigma Press is
based in Wilmslow, to where Romany moved in 1939 to be nearer to the BBC
studios in Manchester. Wilmslow was chosen as it was then a leafy suburb,
with plenty of opportunities for studying wildlife. Romany's caravan is located
near to Wilmslow Library and can be visited on the second Saturday in the
month, from May to September, 12.00 noon to 3.00pm.]*

From the farm accompany the fence to a gate; walk round the edge of the
wood and then carry on across the field. Continue to follow the fence past
the wood to reach a gap in the hedge. Go straight ahead to ascend the gentle
slope and follow the faint track to the right-hand gate. Pass a copse and a
pond on the left and take the route between two fences alongside a planta-

tion to meet a gate. Bear left following the boundary fence and notice a glimpse of Kirkoswald Castle half-hidden by trees. Keep straight on passing massive oak trees on a hillside terrace in very pleasant surroundings. Proceed to a gate on the left side of the castle moat and follow the fence and hedge to a gate, step stile and footpath sign.

Kirkoswald Castle was built in about the year 1200 by Ranulph d'Engayne; it was subsequently enlarged, crenellated and a deer park enclosed by Sir Hugh de Morville, who is not to be confused with one of Thomas à Becket's murderers.

In 1314 the castle was destroyed by the Scots; later rebuilt by the de Multon family and further strengthened by the construction of a ditch. The manor of Kirkoswald passed to the Dacres and the great hall and chapel were built by Thomas Lord Dacre. In 1604 Lord William Howard proceeded to dismantle the building and the stones and timber were sold; this very impressive castle was reduced to a bare shell at the end of the seventeenth century.

All that remains of the castle today is a rather unsafe tower standing on the north side that included a spiral staircase. There is also evidence that the fortress was of a rectangular design with two tunnel vaulted angle towers on the south side. Much of the moat is preserved, but sadly the site is badly overgrown with rampant undergrowth and nettles.

Turn left down the lane noticing the separate church tower on the hill top in front. At the road junction there's an interesting looking building on the right with an inscribed lintel above a former doorway – THOMAS EVS BENET 1622. If you walk round the corner, the house displays a very fine Georgian facade, with ten window lights and two flights of steps leading to a fine doorway. The road continues down the slope to cross the Raven Beck and into the village of Kirkoswald for refreshment facilities.

From the road junction go straight ahead passing the College on the right and the entrance to the village church, which is dedicated to St Oswald. The handsome old College was founded in 1523 by Thomas de Dacre and his wife and was lived in by working clergy until the Dissolution. The College is now a private house, the home of the Fetherstonhaugh family.

Continue down the road to reach a gate and stile just before the Eden Bridge. This elegant sandstone built structure spans the river with two large and small arches. It was built in 1762 to link the villages of Lazonby and Kirkoswald.

Follow the hedge for a little way to reach a copse of Scots pine and a gate. Pass through and keep by the hedge to meet a stone bridge. Carry straight on along the riverside track. Beyond two stone pillars there's a small wooden hut on the right. Proceed over a step stile at a bend and forge ahead along a lovely stretch of riverbank. Walk towards a gate and a footpath sign to meet

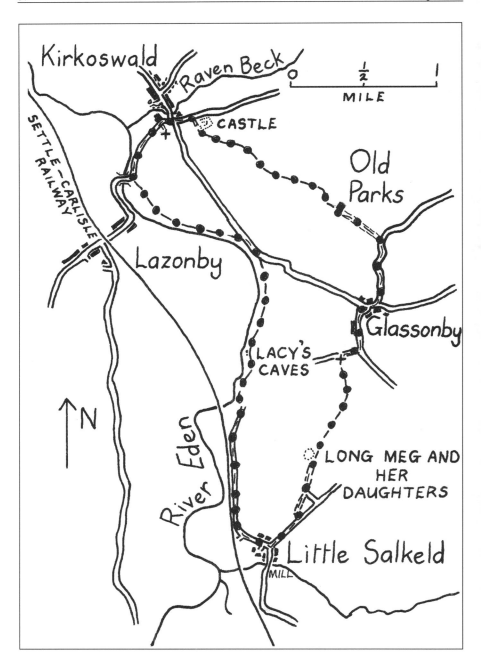

the road. Bear right for a short distance, cross Daleraven Bridge then take the footpath on the right.

The route heads through trees to a step stile and across a field at a good height above the river. Descend to cross a boggy patch and go forward to reach a stile on the river bank. Further on negotiate a broken stile leading into woodland. Here, a number of planks and footbridges assist progress across wet areas. Beyond, there are patches of butterbur and Indian balsam.

Continue through the woods with the going now much better underfoot. The surroundings are idyllic with areas of mature pine and broadleaf trees. There are rock outcrops on the left as the path runs well above the river. Descend and walk round to the right for Lacy's Caves. Take note of the warning signs and proceed carefully.

The original natural caves were greatly enlarged by Lt. Col. Samuel Lacy who felt that his Salkeld Hall estate would benefit from the promotion of such a feature; another explanation was that he actually intended to use them as wine stores. The caves consist of five large chambers linked by arched entrances and are dark despite having windows cut into the sandstone on the river side.

Return through the rock cutting to the main path and continue through Cave Wood. Ahead, the sound of rushing water is easily heard. At a point where a ruined building lies under the slope, deviate to the right and descend for a very good view of the falls.

Across the river lies Force Mill. In previous days the river powered a corn mill on the one bank and a mine on the other. From medieval times, a packhorse bridge crossed the river but seasonal floods washed away a series of these structures. Looking beyond the falls, the Settle-Carlisle railway crosses the Eden by means of a fine arched bridge.

Pass the site of the closed Long Meg mine and its former extensive railway sidings. The way swings left past an electricity sub-station and reaches a footpath sign; then it turns to the right up the track and bears right again.

Gypsum for Plaster of Paris and anhydrite for sulphuric acid were extracted from this area. Sulphate of lime or Gypsum is a sedimentary rock precipitated from evaporating sea water under dry or arid conditions in the Permian era. The Permian Rocks are red sandstones associated with magnesium limestone apparently deposited in inland salt lakes.

Proceed along the former mine road which accompanies the railway almost into the village of Little Salkeld. There are pleasant views across the green Eden Valley. In the village, at the foot of the hill on the Langwathby road, lies Little Salkeld Watermill which is open to visitors.

Bear left at the road junction and walk to the village limits. Take the track on the left to join a metalled lane. Proceed over a cattle grid and forward to the site of the stone circle called Long Meg and Her Daughters.

Long Meg and some of her daughters

The circle dates to the Neolithic/Early Bronze Age and comprises an outlier of red sandstone and a ring of geologically different boulders – her daughters. There are about sixty-six stones set in a rough oval and the tallest stone, Long Meg, is a 15ft (4.57m) column of sandstone. At the point closest to Long Meg, four stones form a porch of two stones along each side. Although the arrangement does not seem to fit into an astronomical alignment, Long Meg is in exactly the right position for the midwinter sun to set over the tall stone. The carvings of cup and ring marks, spirals and concentric circles that decorate Long Meg are usually found in other sites with a mainly funerary purpose.

Follow a BW past the southern edge of the circle to a gap in the fence and walk along the side of the hedgerow to reach a gate. An arrow points to the right of the wall, so continue to a small gate and pass a plantation on the right. There are two more gates to negotiate, before arriving at another gate leading into a farm drive. Carry straight on and proceed down the field to St

Michael's Church, with its well-kept graveyard containing part of an eleventh century cross. This interesting church which seems to have fifteenth century chancel windows, stands apart from the village of Glassonby and is known as Addingham Church. It replaced the medieval building washed away in floods when the Eden changed its course.

Turn right and walk down the track. On reaching the road bear left and proceed for a short distance to the starting point in Glassonby.

Armathwaite and along the banks of the River Eden

Route:	Armathwaite, Drybeck, Edenbrows Woods, Cote House, Wetheral Woods, St Constantine's Cells, Wetheral
Distance:	8½ miles (13.6km) linear walk
Highest Elevation:	Cote House 246ft (75m)
Total ascent:	243ft (74m)
Maps:	1:25000 Explorer OL Nos. 315 and 5; 1:50000 Landranger No. 86.
How to get there:	A6 north of Penrith to High Hesket Old Town, side road to Armathwaite. Or, from A69 via B6263 to Wetheral and side road to Armathwaite
Starting point:	Armathwaite grid reference NY 5060 4610
Finishing point:	Wetheral grid reference NY 4680 5466
Terrain:	Paths through riverside pastures and woodland

The place name Armathwaite means 'The clearing of the hermit'. In 1232 it was known as Ermitethwayt. The suffix thwaite from Old Scandinavian means a clearing.

The village lies in a peaceful hollow close to the wide and smooth flowing River Eden. For lengthy sections of the river hereabouts, the banksides are clothed with trees and overlooked by sandstone outcrops. The river is spanned here by a graceful bridge built in 1908; it is the only road crossing between Warwick Bridge and Lazonby. The river is not only famous for its riverside scenery but also for the quality of its salmon fishing. There are two inns that cater for the needs of thirsty anglers, namely, The Duke's Head on the west bank and the Fox and Pheasant on the east.

Armathwaite Castle, now converted to flats, was the home of the Skelton family whose influence in the district went back to the reign of Edward II. King Edward IV granted the family land on the banks of the Eden and the castle and surrounding woodland was owned by the Skeltons until 1712. The castle was originally a pele tower, but its appearance was changed over the years, and substantially altered by the introduction of a Georgian facade. In the mid-nineteenth century it was purchased by the 2nd Earl of Lonsdale and sold again in 1888.

The village church of Christ and St Mary is a small unpretentious building on high ground overlooking the river. It seems very surprising that it was once in a dilapidated condition having been used as a cattle byre. The building consists of a nave and chancel all in one and lit by small round-headed windows.

Armathwaite is fortunate to have a railway station on the Settle to Carlisle line that is open and in use for local residents and tourists.

The Walk

From the small triangular area just past the Post Office, bear left and follow the road uphill to reach the access path to the church. By the roadside is a sandstone building which was presented by W H Woodhouse Esq. in 1854; it is now being used as the Village Hall and Parish Rooms. The Wetheral road is a quiet rural route running parallel to the river and railway. Pass Quarry House, and continue on the road to meet a group of houses and farm buildings at Lockhills. A little further on there's a cottage with a walled garden and a railway viaduct to the rear.

Proceed to the farm road on the right, then passing the lodge and the entrance to the drive into parkland leading to Low House. Keep straight on as the access road swings left by a farm wall. Here, there is a good view of Low House which has a massive bank of chimneys. The walled lane with a verge of ferns and bracken now turns towards the river. The surroundings are leafy and verdant as the route passes a large island in mid stream.

Leave the lane and continue along the path, passing through a canopy of beech, alder, birch, ash and the occasional Spanish chestnut. Dappled sunlight falls on a riot of Himalayan balsam, nettles and bracken alongside the clear path. All around there are beautiful vistas of the river, from a sandstone cliff on the left, coloured a rich red-brown, to the steep wooded slopes on the far bank. Approach a small kissing gate with an access to the riverside meadow. However, a notice proclaims: NO ACCESS TO RIVERBANK. KEEP TO FOOTPATH. Pass a small railed hut opposite to Hawkcliffe Scar which lies on the far river bank. There are good waymarkers here with yellow topped posts. Approach a wire fence and footpath sign and bear left up the slope to a step stile. Walk along the edge of the field and come to a stile in the fence.

Continue through the pasture alongside the fence with wooded slopes on the right dropping down to the river. Keep going to a step stile and a notice with more reading material: FOLLOW FENCE. PLEASE DO NOT CUT ACROSS FIELD CORNERS. Looking to the left, there is the farm complex of Wallace Field. Pass through a step stile, go for a short distance along the edge of a wooded section; and if you are lucky, locate the footpath sign which was, on the last visit, stuck up a tree. Descend the little depression and then bear left on a slope through the trees. The Eden is flowing more rapidly now

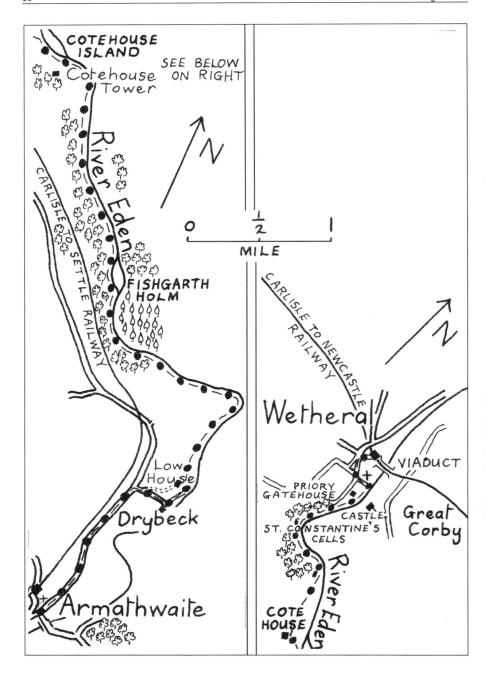

through rocky channels, as you continue along the river bank passing lichen and moss-covered boulders.

Approach a step stile over a fence and pass a finger post. There's an interesting destination on one arm, namely Froddle Crook: it certainly is a name to stir the imagination. Proceed along the riverside path through trees, lush vegetation and a profusion of balsam, or whatever the collective noun is for a lot of that particular flower. Pass a WM and arrive at a small, green painted hut on stilts – Eden Bros Top Hut: a building no doubt reserved for froddling fisherpersons. Ascend a little above the river to walk along a lovely section of path, and then descend to reach another hut. Now, what with a Froddle Crook, a green hut on stilts, and a sinister, black, wire-mesh fronted structure with a truck on rails inside, we almost have a plot for a good mystery story.

Walk over a track and continue straight on through the trees. Cross a footbridge and pass through trees and undergrowth, with the river channel on the right to meet a step stile over a fence. Keep to the edge of the field.

The river continues to flow rapidly over a wide bed against a background of tree-covered cliffs. Go past another fishing hut, and across the field on the left is a wooded area with a derelict stone building between the trees.

Descend to cross a small watercourse and carry on along the field edge. Stride over an electric fence, fairly low fortunately for the less-agile fraternity , and walk along the riverside meadow. Proceed through a gap passing a redundant stile to a footbridge over a ditch, and go forward to negotiate another ditch to reach a yellow-topped pole. Continue to a step stile to pass a broad stretch of the river at this point. Go over a plank footbridge and carry on between trees

The route descends to cross another plank and heads through a neatly sawn gap in a fallen tree. Whilst taking a breather, it was fascinating to hear the eerie creaking sound emanating from the tall trees as they moved in the wind.

Beyond this point the path crosses a plank footbridge, a patch of butterbur and a brick structure with a pipe in the ground. Ahead, the way includes a number of plank footbridges and step stiles on a well-marked route to reach a large tombstone. Matthew Knublay was a local quarryman who made this headstone for his parents; but as they were buried elsewhere; and Matthew was not allowed to remove it from the parish, so he erected the stone where it is today.

Continue over stiles along the river bank and note the odd-looking house on the hillside terrace. It has a square tower and a shallow pitched roof and could be regarded as the precursor for a Victorian railway station. In reality, Coathouse or Cote House Tower was built in the 1840s to act as an observation post to keep watch for illegal salmon fishing.

Keep straight on by Coathouse Island and traverse left up the grass slope following waymarkers; and then ascend through the trees to reach a step stile in the fence opposite Cote House Farm. Bear right to a footpath sign by a gate and stile; the end walls of the farmhouse, is in fact, the remains of a pele tower. Walk down the track descending gradually, with a pleasant park-like aspect in front, and approach Wetheral Pumping Station standing amidst a splendid riverside scene.

Meet a kissing gate and pass a National Trust notice indicating WETHERAL WOODS. The route passes through lovely leafy surroundings, which is noted for its rich variety of ground covering flowers and plants. Proceed on a well-maintained path to reach a storage hut on the left.

Ahead lies the sandstone cliff face containing St Constantine's Cells. Begin to ascend to a point high above the river and then a path descends a little to negotiate a flight of rock cut steps leading to the man-made caves. The three chambers linked by a passage are thought to pre-date Roman times, and are believed to be later associated with St Constantine, the local patron saint. There's much evidence of graffiti, ancient and modern, with an interesting inscription close to the cells carved by William H. Mounsey in 1852. The words reflect a verse from the songs of a ninth century Welsh poet. Mounsey was responsible for other inscriptions nearer the river, and is thought to be the sculptor for the large enigmatic faces on the sandstone cliffs of the Eden gorge near Armathwaite.

Turn about, ascend the steps, and take the route that descends the slope, and continues to the lower path when the route forks. A weir may be seen on the far side of the river as this lower path keeps to the riverside to meet a kissing gate. Proceed ahead along a fenced path with terraced gardens on the far bank of the river. These are part of the grounds of Corby Castle.

Looking in front there's a glimpse of Wetheral, and a splendid view of the famous railway viaduct. Descend a flight of stone steps opposite the handsome building of the castle perched high on the cliffs. Below the big house are caves in the sandstone, but the pleasant aspect is rather spoiled by the sight of a considerable length of uniform metal railings; it appears that some of the local residents are not too pleased either. Also, on the far bank is the cottage where the ferryboat used to operate from until the late 1950s.

Turn left and ascend on the road to reach the church dedicated to The Holy Trinity and St Constantine, with its neat octagonal tower and beautifully tended churchyard. The exterior of the building is early sixteenth century, although the layout of the church, apart from the tower, was in the fourteen century. A square tower was added to the church in 1760, and this was replaced in 1882.

Attached to the north side of the chancel is the Howard Chapel, c.1791, above the family vault of the Howard family of Corby Castle. The red sand-

Wetheral Cross and Green

stone chapel was built to house a beautiful, white marble statue as a memorial to Lady Maria Howard who died in childbirth together with her baby daughter in November 1789. This sculpture by Joseph Nollekens (R.A. 1732-1823) is regarded as one of his best works.

Continue up the road to arrive at the Green.

Taking the road to the left, it is only a short walk to reach the site of the Benedictine Priory founded in 1100 by Ranulph de Meschines. Many grants and rich endowments made the priory a wealthy and prosperous place; it employed the villagers in and about the priory, on the land, in the mill and in fishing. The priory was a place of sanctuary, a privilege granted by Henry I in his Charter of Rights. Following the Dissolution of the Monasteries it eventually passed to the Dean and Chapter of Carlisle.

Today, all that remains of the priory is the fine gatehouse, which has been well-restored by the National Trust. **Note:** The gatehouse can also be reached by continuing on the upper path after the visit to St Constantine's Cells.

The handsome grassy area enhances the centre of the village. It used to be a piece of common land grazed by sheep and other animals. A maypole once stood there, then it was resited at the south-eastern corner, and finally was replaced by the present stone cross.

Pass a hotel on the right, and a licensed restaurant on the left across the Green. At the far end turn right and walk down the road past the Crown Hotel to reach Wetheral Station. Now at the end of the day you may wish to catch a train, but you may also wish to walk across the viaduct for a spectacular crossing of the Eden.

Cross the railway footbridge, pass down the station platform, and walk on the iron footbridge that runs alongside the viaduct. There are magnificent views to be gained, and the walk across and back should not be missed.

Note: Wetheral viaduct consists of five 80ft (24.3m) arches, 100ft (30.4m) high. Built 1831-1834. Francis Giles, civil engineer, William Denton, builder.

Askham to Morland through pastoral Westmorland

Route:	Askham, Lowther Castle, Newtown, Lowther, Hackthorpe, Melkinthorpe, Great Strickland, Field Head, Lansmere Farm, Greengill Sike, Morland
Distance:	8¾ miles (14km) linear walk
Highest Elevation:	Field Head 689ft (210m)
Total ascent:	509ft (155m)
Maps:	1:25000 Explorer OL Nos. 5 and 19; 1:50000 Landranger Nos 90 and 91.
How to get there:	Leave A6 at Hackthorpe and by road to Askham or from Eamont Bridge (Penrith M6), A6, take B5320 to Yanwath and side road to Askham
Starting point:	Askham; grid reference 5120 2365
Finishing point:	Morland; grid reference 6000 2235
Terrain:	A gentle undulating landscape of pastures, streams, hedgerows and woodland. N.B. This walk follows the route of The Ravenber – a coast to coast long distance walk from Ravenglass to Berwick-upon-Tweed [the whole journey is described by the author in a guide book published by Landmark Publishing, 2003].

Askham, the settlement of ash trees, has long laid claim to be the prettiest village in the district. There are a number of attractive stone dwellings of the seventeenth and eighteenth centuries; date stones 1650-1763. The houses and cottages are set at interesting angles and many are white and colour washed with painted door and window mouldings. The wide tree-lined grass verges are splashed with snowdrops, crocuses and daffodils in spring-time.

Askham Hall is the ancient manor house of the Lowther Estate and has been the home of the Earl of Lonsdale since the dismantling of Lowther Castle. The massive pele tower and adjoining parts are of the fourteenth century but the remaining sections of the house are of the seventeenth or early eighteenth century. The Hall is a spacious building with three irregular wings set round an oblong courtyard.

The Walk

As you descend the main street passing The Punchbowl Inn, look to the left

Askham

through the gateway to Askham Hall. Beyond its encircling high stone wall there are fine examples of topiary to be seen in front of the house and in February the grassy borders are carpeted with snowdrops.

The road dips down to the gracefully arched Askham Bridge spanning the River Lowther. To the right, St Peter's Church lies in a leafy setting on the banks of the river. It was built in 1832 on the site of an earlier building and has a plain interior with no stained glass. The south transept is much older and was originally the chapel of the Sandford family who lived at Askham Hall from 1375 until 1680.

The church of St Michael lies up the road from Askham Bridge. Its monuments to the Lowther family and the Earls of Lonsdale are of much interest. There are hog-back coffins in the porch and in the churchyard the Lowther Mausoleum, c.1857, contains the white seated figure of William 2nd Earl of Lonsdale. The church has a twelfth century arcade and generally the building was altered to unusual proportions in 1696 and 1856.

As the road swings left at Askham Bridge take the path on the right which climbs up through the trees overlooking the river. NOTE: There is no recorded right of way along this short length of path although it is marked footpath on the 1916 O.S. map; it is an obvious link into the rights of way network, i.e. footpath 34200 and footpath 342008. There is a possibility that

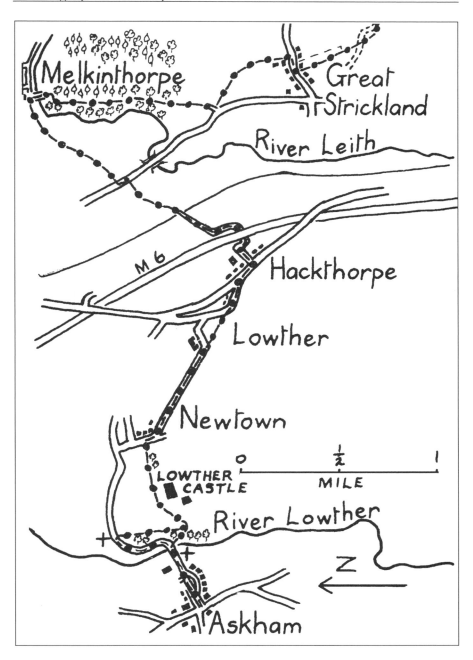

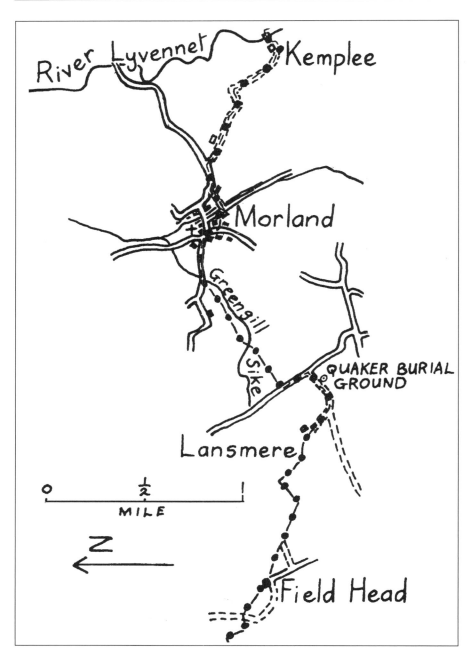

this link may be dedicated as a public footpath, or at least a permissive route. If this permission is not granted then the alternative is to walk up the road and take the right of way, footpath No. 342006 opposite the entrance to St Michael's Church. Proceed through Castlesteads Plantation to meet the route in question at the top of the wooded slope. This will add a good half a mile onto the distance from Askham to Morland.

Walk towards the high wall surrounding Lowther Castle.

The castle occupies the site of earlier mansions dating back to the reign of Henry II. Now a hollow shell, this mighty Gothic-style building was begun in 1806 and completed in 1811 after the previous building had burned down in 1720. From 1880 to 1944, the title, Earl of Lonsdale was held by Hugh. He was a great sportsman who left the famous Lonsdale belts for boxing. His favourite colour was yellow and also the colour of the Automobile Association, of which he was their first president.

The greater part of Lowther Castle was demolished in 1957 but the remaining facade presents a wonderfully varied skyline; an array of symmetrical, turreted and embattled shapes.

Walk past the gatehouse, which gives the appearance of being heavily fortified, to meet a gate. Continue ahead and follow a line of trees towards a row of houses. From a ladder stile pass between two forlorn looking stone gateposts to reach the road. Newtown was an early effort at town planning when, in 1685, Sir John Lowther demolished the old village and began the building of Lowther New Town.

Turn right and follow the road as it swings left and continue for a mile along this quiet country way. Take heart, a welcoming sign soon appears – TEA ROOM AND LAKELAND BIRD GARDEN, tel: 01931 712746.

There is a glimpse of the distant Pennines as one approaches Lowther village; it is certainly the work of Robert Adam, (1728-1792), with an attractive layout of two closes joined on the north side with a seven bay, two storey house, and complete with water pump and trough.

Directly in front, on the angle of the sharp bend, is a stile in the wall followed by a short stretch of footpath. Proceed along the road passing a primary school to meet the junction with the main road.

Hackthorpe, old Norse, Haki's Thorp – Haki's settlement or farm, is a village divided by the A6. This is undoubtedly Lowther country, even the inn is named after the famous family, while the village school has the Lowther shield cut into the sandstone fabric. Hackthorpe Hall which stands at the southern end of the village is a splendid Jacobean farmhouse with mullioned windows. The artist Jacob Thompson, (1806-1879), lived in the village during the latter years of his life. He is remembered for such works as "Agony in the Garden", "Angels appearing to the Shepherds", "Drawing the Net at Hawes Water" and "The Rush Bearers".

Cross the main road, pass the post office and turn left down a farm track which bends under the motorway. Bear left to walk parallel with it, before turning away to the right and down to a sandstone bridge crossing the main railway line. The track ends here, but proceed ahead along the right-hand side of the hedge. The line of the path is not clear but where the hedge bends slightly go through a gate and aim for another gate in front. Now walk down the field to a gate at the bottom with power lines crossing overhead. Turn left along Waterfalls Road for a short distance to a gate on the right.

Follow the hedge to a gate and continue down a sunken grassy way meeting some waterlogged sections. Some farm buildings appear on the left. At a small fenced-off area of the track go left through a gate and follow the hedgerow down the field. Turn right by the first dwelling on the edge of the hamlet of Melkinthorpe. Cross the footbridge over the River Leith, continue for a short way and then bear right at a track junction. The BW leads through Melkinthorpe Wood, which is a pleasant tract of mixed woodland containing oak, willow, birch and conifer. The bridleway reaches an area of rhododendrons by a gate.

Proceed straight ahead to a gate and continue with a hedge on the left to another gate. The track then passes through a third gate beyond to meet a minor road. On the left, a footpath sign indicates the direction of the route to Great Strickland. The land has been cleared of timber and the path heads diagonally across the area to follow the left-hand side of a fence to a stile. Enter a field for a few paces to a stile in the hedge on the left. Walk through the fields to a gate before the farm. Pass a barn on the right to a second gate and continue ahead to the road at Great Strickland. Turn right towards the centre of the village.

Great Strickland; Magna Stirkeland or Styrkeland, Old English, styrc – land or pasture for young bullocks or heifers.

The village is situated in an entirely agricultural landscape between the A6 and the River Eden. The villages, hamlets and farmsteads are quiet places served by a network of country lanes, such as Priestclose, Aisygill and Maudy. Great Strickland is served by a church, chapel and a post office and the Strickland Arms provides bar meals.

Just a short distance along the road the existing path, No. 325001, indicated by a footpath sign, is subject to a diversion order. The proposed new route will start a little further up the road and will join the current route at the far end of a long thin field. The existing way proceeds through a farmyard, continues across a large field to a stile in the right-hand corner and then bears sharp right round the end of a long thin field. This is the point where the proposed diversion route will link up. Walk to a gate, then left through a stone stile and along a fence into Maudy Lane. The land is actually a track at this point.

Go through a gate and across to another gate on the right. Keep on a diagonal route to a gate and a flimsy stile. Bear left and follow the semblance of a green track to another gate. Head to the right alongside a fence, then turn left at a wall and accompany it to a stile.

Cross the farm lane, then through a couple of wall stiles and up the meadow to Field Head, where the farmyard is entered and exited via three metal gates. Beyond the farm take the right-hand gate on the left and go diagonally across the field to a stile leading into a lane. Pass through a gate and follow the fence boundary that includes a few trees and thorn bushes; this in turn becomes a stone wall leading to a gate near ponds. Turn left and follow the wall climbing steadily; then head right and keep alongside the fence to a lone ash tree and a gate. Proceed across a small field to a gate and keep by the fence which is succeeded by a wall.

The route heads towards Lansmere Farm and continues through the farmyard with two gates to become a wide clear track. Note a stile to the right, which gives access to the site of a Quaker Burial Ground. This secluded walled enclosure contains a number of old gravestones. Of particular interest is a stone with an inscription in Latin. This is supported by a tablet carrying an English translation, with both stones sheltered under a canopy.

When the track meets the road, turn left and walk for a short distance to a gate on the right, with a footpath sign to Morland. Descend gently to a gate on the left, across to a stile and down to the corner of the field near a stream gully. From the stile cross Greengill Sike, climb up the opposite bank and follow a hedge to a couple of stiles. Bear right round a depression to cross a wire fence with a yellow WM on a nearby tree. Morland village now comes into view. There is a deep gully on the right with young trees and a little stream. Descend to a footpath sign and a large slab of stone through a stone wall. Walk up the lane into Morland village.

Proceed straight ahead to a footpath sign on the left. Descend behind houses, over a small ladder stile then between hedges to stone steps and into a cobbled yard. The building on the right was previously the Kings Arms Inn. However, don't worry there's the Crown Inn in the village square.

Morland and Crossrigg

Route:	Morland, River Lyvennet, Crossrigg, Winter House, Morland.
Distance:	4.5 miles (7.2km) circular walk.
Highest Elevation:	377ft (115m) road near Highgate Farm
Maps:	1:25000 Explorer OL Nos. 5 and 19; 1:50000 Landranger No. 91.
How to get there:	Leave A66 at Temple Sowerby and side roads via Ousenstand Bridge, Lane End and Lyvennet Bridge to Morland.
Start/Finish Point	Morland, footbridge over Morland Beck, grid reference NY 600 223
Terrain:	Gently undulating countryside and riverside pastures.

In 1140 the settlement's name was Morlund, which means, 'the grove by the moor'. The element 'lund' is from the Old Norse, lundr, meaning a grove or copse.

The village slopes down to the gently flowing Morland Beck in the lovely Vale of Lyvennet. The village stream, Morland Beck, is crossed by a long, white-painted footbridge and a ford. The stream has a colony of resident ducks.

The Walk

Cross over the footbridge, and walk straight ahead up the lane. The road gently descends to cross Lyvennet Bridge in wooded surroundings. Take the path, WM, on the right, into the wood, which slants up through the trees to reach a step stile, WM . Cross the road to a gate, WM, and continue down the hedged track. The way turns sharp right and then sharp left at a step stile. Proceed along the hedgerow to a step stile, WM, and on to the road.

Turn left and walk along the road to Lane End, and then left again at the road junction. Proceed for a short distance, passing the drive to Crossrigg Farm, and then take the stile in the hedgerow on the right. Walk across the field aiming for a distant electricity supply pole, to reach a step stile in the fence. The route is now on the fine wooded banks above the Lyvennet.

Aim for a step stile in the left-hand corner of the fence, and descend through trees to another step stile in a fence. Continue along the river bank to reach a gate, WM. The large house to the right, set in parkland, is Crossrigg Hall. This is a Victorian Tudor house, very varied in outline, with battlements and mullioned and transomed windows. Walk through the river meadow, and note the splendid stone barn in the field on the opposite bank

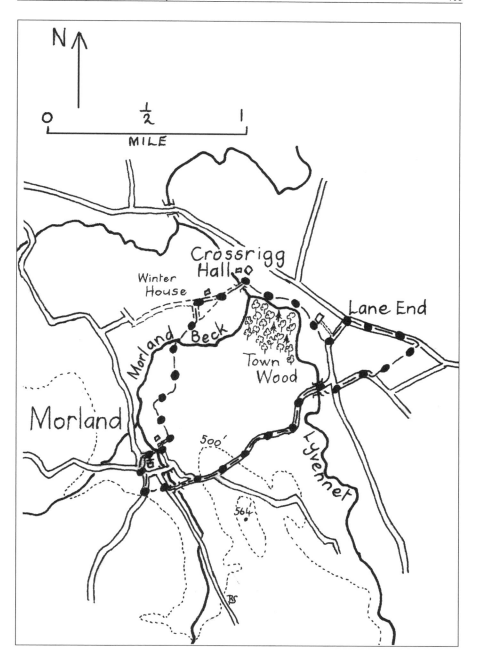

Morland Beck, Morland

of the river. Turn left on reaching the track, and cross over the attractive iron bridge supported on stone pillars. The surroundings are particularly delightful in this sylvan spot – another secret valley.

Follow the track to a gate, WM, and continue between an avenue of mature oaks to a small gate, WM. Pass in front of Winter House, and then bear left at a track junction. You can cut off the corner by using the right of way on the left before Winter House, which goes through an area of young trees.

The track bends to the right and descends between hedgerows full of elderberry bushes. The way is now an old sunken way, a holloway used by travellers from early times. Pass the site of a former dwelling, ignore the WM, on the right, and proceed straight on to cross the footbridge. The way passes between trees, and bends to climb gently amongst more trees and colourful bushes. There is now a view of the neat tower and spire of St. Laurence's Church in Morland. The path turns sharp left, ignore the path off to the right, and continue towards the village. At Little Appleby, the route turns sharp left and meets a footpath on the right. At this point one can either carry straight on along the way, which becomes a lane into the village – attractions being a fine high-spanned bridge and the Crown Inn; or, to turn right at Little Appleby on the path which crosses the beck on a footbridge, and continues alongside the church. Some details about the history of the church may be found at the beginning of the Morland to Dufton Walk, page 106.

Turn left beyond the church on to the road, and walk for a short distance past a road junction. Keep straight ahead and pass a road on the left, and continue to meet a WM on the left. This path descends behind the houses to reach a small ladder stile. Continue between hedges to stone steps and into a cobbled yard to reach the road. Turn right, and walk alongside the beck back to the starting point.

From Morland to Dufton through the Vale of Lyvennet

Route: Morland, Kemplee Farm, Chapel Bridge, Jackdaws' Scar,
                        Kings Meaburn, Bolton, Powis Farm, Trout Beck, Long
                        Marton, Mill Beck, Dufton

Distance: 8 miles (12.8 km) linear walk

Highest Elevation: Dufton 558ft (170m)

Total ascent: 453ft (138m)

Maps: 1:25000 Explorer OL No.19; 1:50000 Landranger No. 91.

How to get there: Leave A66 at Temple Sowerby and side roads via Ousenstand
                        Bridge, Lane End and Lyvennet Bridge to Morland

Starting point: Morland; grid reference NY 6000 2235

Finishing point: Dufton grid reference NY 6895 2505

Terrain: Pleasant pastures, hedgerows and copses of woodland.
                        Attractive stream and river valleys. A crossing of Trout Beck
                        [The Ravenber route]

Morland means 'the grove by a moor'. The village slopes down to the banks of Morland Beck in the lovely Vale of Lyvennet. If there is time to spare, the great attraction is the ancient parish church of St Laurence. This eleventh century building has a number of Anglo Saxon features including the red sandstone tower recognised by the bell openings and the narrow and high doorway to the nave. The tower is capped by a neat lead spire added after a seventeenth century top storey. There is evidence of Norman architecture, plus the fact that the church was probably extended in the late twelfth century. There are Georgian arched windows and a Royal Coat of Arms of George III. A brass memorial commemorates a local vicar, John Blyth, who died in 1562 and another depicting a sixteenth century Knight.

The village stream, Morland Beck, passes under the high spanned bridge near to the Crown Inn. The appropriately named Water Street accompanies the beck and its tranquil unspoiled appearance is enhanced by a long white painted footbridge, a ford and a quota of contented resident ducks.

The Walk

Cross over the footbridge and walk straight ahead up the road to reach a public bridleway sign on the right. A good wide track leads to Kemplee Farm through pleasant open countryside. Pass the farm, cross over Chapel Bridge

The River Eden near Bolton

and bear right along the banks of the River Lyvennet. The leafy slopes are covered with primroses, celandines, daisies, violets and forget-me-nots in springtime. Proceed through the meadow as small rock outcrops appear to the left. The path approaches a stile to be quickly followed by another one to enter Barnholme Wood. Here the river tumbles over its rocky bed and celandines and bluebells carpet the woodland ground.

Negotiate a stile and continue through a lush meadow with the impressive Jackdaws' Scar rising vertically from the valley floor. The crags live up to their name as they are home to real jackdaws.

Walk along the track passing a white painted cottage and two stone gate posts. At this point the lane fords the river and a long footbridge enables pedestrians to keep their feet dry. Turn left and walk up the road, bearing left at the top into Kings Meaburn. The cottages of this small rural community line the road, which also includes a chapel and the White Horse Inn. The village gets its name from an early ownership by the Crown, which seized the estates of the Lord of the Manor, Sir Hugh Morville, for his part in the murder of Thomas a Becket, Archbishop of Canterbury.

Just beyond the inn a footpath sign on the right indicates the way to Bolton. Proceed through two gates with the second one leading into a long narrow field. Descend to cross a stream on wooden planks and walk up to a

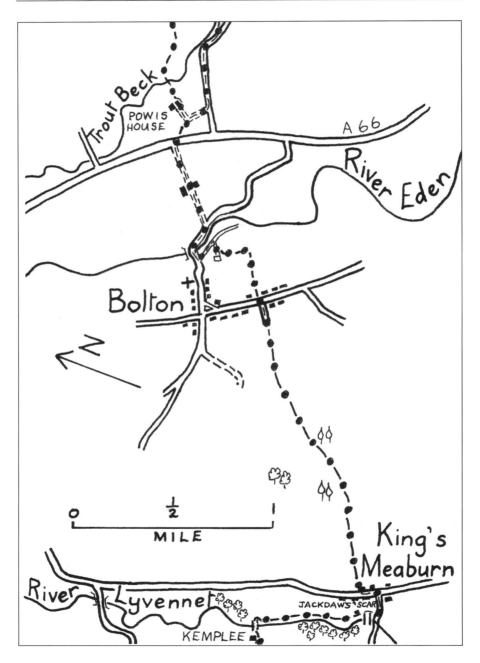

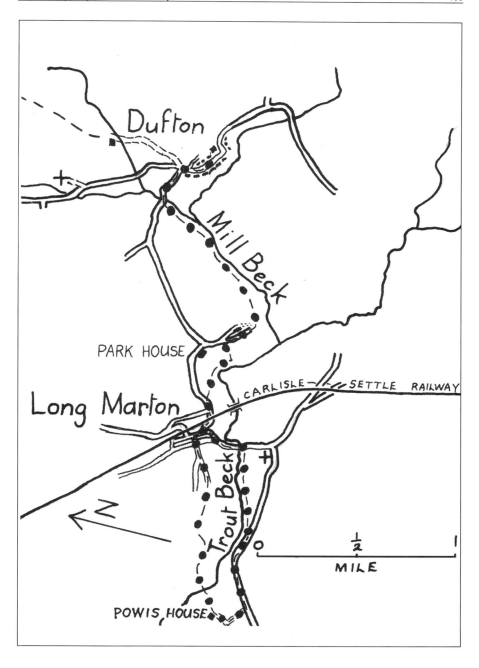

gate. Follow the fence and hedge on the right-hand side, then through a gate to keep the left-hand side of a plantation. Go through the small area of woodland to reach a barbed wire fence. The top strand is covered, but persons who are slight of stature may require some assistance from a convenient stone.

Continue along the right-hand side of a hedge to a gate and then forward to a stile in a stone wall. Follow the hedge to a corner with a stone gap stile. The village of Bolton is now in sight, as the route aims diagonally to a stile near a metal water trough. Walk alongside the fence to a gate, cross a stream by means of two large stones and aim slightly left to a hedge gap with a stone step. Proceed up the hedge side to a small gate in the corner and take the track ahead leading to a metal gate. Continue past the farm to another gate and onto the road. A footpath sign points to Kings Meaburn.

Persons desiring refreshments at the New Crown Inn, or to view the lovely All Saints Church should turn left at this point, grid reference NY 6395 2290.

Cross the road to a footpath sign indicating Bolton Mill. Enter a small trackway to a gate and go on for a few paces to a stile. Walk down the field towards a simple stile which is situated near to a gate. Bear left through a small area of young trees and follow the hedgerow to the left with an elevated view across the valley. Keep to the faint path alongside a fence, passing gorse bushes, to reach a stile. There's another stile further on to the right leading into a field. Just take a few strides and then turn left to walk round the sewage works perimeter fence to a gate.

Note: Due to previous building work on the site, the right of way is unclear. The path should follow the hedgerow straight ahead but there is an unstiled fence across the route. An alternative is to turn down the works track to a gate, go left and proceed along the metalled lane to Bolton Bridge. There the footpath sign is in situ pointing the way beyond a fastened-up gate along the line of the hedgerow.

Walk over the fine twin-arched Bolton Bridge spanning the River Eden and then along the road for a short distance, before turning left on the BW to Redlands Bank Farm. The track climbs gently passing the farm buildings to meet the A66. Bear right and walk a few paces along the grass verge; it's time for a quick dash across to the other side of this busy main road. A footpath sign indicates the way to Long Marton; the path through the field actually crosses the corner edge of a Roman camp. A concrete ladder stile leads on to the track bed of the old Eden Valley Railway. Turn right and walk only a short distance to a bungalow. Take the stile on the left and go straight on down the farm drive to Powis House.

Approach the farm and continue round the building on the right to meet the corner of the hedge on the far side. Walk along the left-hand side of the hedge then descend left to the side of the Trout Beck.

This footpath route, No. 341 017, has been the subject of representations to the Rights of Way Officer responsible for the area. After discussion and further correspondence the latest situation is as follows: the barbed wire will be removed either side of Trout Beck and beyond and stiles will be installed. The beck will have to be forded. The question of a bridge will be considered at a later date.

This seems to be a very worthwhile project that the Ramblers' Association, Rambling Clubs and Affiliated Bodies could be involved in helping to get the bridge installed. This is an important linking footpath route across the Eden Valley.

Ford the fairly wide stream, which can be appreciably full in wintertime, and climb up the opposite bank. Keep on up the left-hand side of the fence to reach a gate. Turn right passing a conifer plantation, pass through a gate and continue through two more gates. Beyond a copse of pines and oaks the track swings left to reach what was a double barricade of barbed wire. If this obstacle has been removed then it is a great relief to walkers. Slant to the right and walk along the right-hand side of the fence to meet a gate. A track now leads to a lane which continues as a metalled surface, passing a small housing development and on into the centre of Long Marton. Turn right at the road junction and walk towards the stone building at the fork in the road.

Alternative Route:

If the thought of fording Trout Beck on a cold morning acts as a deterrent then there is an alternative, which involves some road walking. This is all the more reason to keep on making representations to Cumbria County Council at Kendal. Note: If you carefully examine the 2½ inches O.S. map you will notice that the beck has at one time been bridged.

After leaving the old railway track bed near to Powis House, walk down the farm drive to the road. Turn left and proceed to a footpath sign situated just beyond the bend in the road. Follow the path, which also had obstructions and where new stiles have been installed, along the top of the stream bank. Continue along the beckside to the road then turn left and walk into Long Marton. (Long Marton, Old English, Mere-Tun or Maer-Tun. (tun) by a lake, the farmstead with a pool.)

This village has dwellings on either side of its quiet main street. The parish of Long Marton stretches onto the Pennine moors beyond Knock Fell to terminate between two tributaries of the Tees.

Many of the houses in the village are built of the local red sandstone, as is the parish church of St Margaret and St James. This lovely interesting building which is situated to the south of the village, has a large twelfth-century tower and two sets of ancient carved stones. Probably Saxon in origin, the one above the south doorway is a tympanum depicting a winged ox in a boat, a dragon and a winged shield charged with a cross.

The north-east corner of the graveyard contains several graves of gypsies who died whilst attending the Appleby Horse Fair. This well-known event is still held every June on Fair Hill to the north of the town.

The Settle-Carlisle railway runs through the village and a battle by pro-railway enthusiasts prevented its closure. The railway has tremendous tourist potential and I fail to comprehend why the village's station platforms were taken out of use. Surely, with the inadequacy of rural transport, a station would benefit the needs of both local people and visitors alike. The village is a useful base for good walking in the Eden Valley and on the nearby Pennines.

Bear left along the Dufton road noting the stone building on the corner. The Parish Institute, built in 1893 enjoyed the facilities of a games room, reading room and assembly room. Pass under the railway bridge and descend to a row of railway cottages. Keep to the right at a footpath sign and head down a grassy lane to a gate. Spare a moment to gaze at the hills in the distance, with a particularly fine view of Dufton Pike.

Note: Representations were made about the lack and state of stiles along footpaths 341 026 and 341 027. I believe that four stiles have now been installed.

Continue across a small field to a stile, pass close to the stream and go ahead to two more stiles. Then bear left and walk up the boundary hedge to reach a gate. Turn right along a track below Park Farm, through two gates, into a walled enclosure and on to a gate. Proceed along the track between thorn bushes to another gate. Cross a narrow meadow and another intake field to reach a stile. Aim ahead for the left-hand corner of the pasture to meet a stile close to the beck.

The charming little valley of Mill Beck under the wooded slopes of Park Brow is a scenic gem and should on no account be missed. The delightful leafy surroundings, the soft gurgling of the stream and numerous wild flowers, combine to create a stunning contrast to the wild Pennine moors.

Head for the corner of the hedge by the beck to reach a stile and an old plank. Proceed to a gate in front but do not cross the beck on the rickety bridge.

The valley narrows to a path on the bankside above the stream and aims for a stile in a wall and towards a small conifer plantation. Continue on a high level path to a shaky stile and then between a stream and a stagnant pond. Follow a wall to a gate and footpath sign; turn right, walk over Mill Bridge and up the road to Dufton.

Section 4: The Pennines

Whilst travelling along the Eden Valley, the eye is constantly drawn to the escarpment of the high Pennines; a barrier which has such a dominating influence on the surrounding countryside. Many of the settlements that are situated at the foot of the eastern fellsides have adapted to their remote positions and have assumed a character all of their own. Most of the houses and cottages are stoutly constructed of red sandstone, and have their backs to the fell as well as to the surrounding pastures. Not only do they have the parochial blasts of the Helm Wind to contend with at certain times of the year, but during the unsettled Border times they were frequently raided by the Scots. A number of these communities, like Milburn, still maintain their medieval form. This consists of a central Green with the dwellings fitting closely together and looking inwards on to the enclosure. Access to the centre of the village was by means of narrow entrances that could easily be defended.

The Pennines reach their highest points in this area, and access to the high tops can be made from several of the fellside villages. Cross Fell, 2930ft (893m) can be climbed from Dufton on the Pennine Way and from Knock, Milburn, Blencarn, Kirkland or Townhead Ousby.

On a clear day the effort is well worthwhile, for the high watershed is an excellent viewpoint, ranging from the superb panorama of Lakeland mountains to the hills of southern Scotland.

A Roman road, the Maiden Way, can be traced to lonely Meg's Cairn on the escarpment edge, and continues across Melmerby Fell in a north-easterly direction. From Meg's Cairn the walk traverses the stony plateau of Stony Rigg, before descending the ancient corpse road to Kirkland.

Dufton is also the starting point for the next stage of The Ravenber long distance walk from Ravenglass to Berwick-upon-Tweed, via Dunfell Hush and Trout Beck to Garrigill.

To the south-east of Dufton lies the village of Hilton, and walkers who desire a variation on the existing routes in the area should attempt the walk up Scordale. See details for Wild Scordale and High Cup Walk, page 137.

The main A686 road struggles over the Hartside Pass, and hereabouts are grassy fells that afford some good remote walking. East of the River Eden, as green pastures and woodland copses gradually give way to the foothills of the high moors, the villages of Renwick and Croglin are ideally situated to explore the King's Forest of Geltsdale. The two villages are quiet, peaceful places, but in the past, both were associated with strange events. The surroundings grouse moors are very fine indeed, with acres of heather,

East fellsides from Blencarn

bilberry, rough grasses and bracken stretching away to the high moorland ridges on the skyline.

The Eller Beck quickly joins the New Water, and the view up this wild valley is reminiscent of the Cheviot Hills. A clear right of way threads through this lovely area which eventually descends towards green pastures and woodland. Here the River Gelt surges onwards down a rapidly deepening valley.

Cross Fell – highest point in the Pennines

Route:	Blencarn, Cringle Moor, Wildboar Scar, Tees Head, Cross Fell, Stoop Band, Hanging Walls Of Mark Anthony, Kirkland, Blencarn
Distance:	11 miles (17.6 km) circular walk
Highest Elevation:	Cross Fell, 2930ft (893m)
Total ascent:	2372ft (723m)
Maps:	1:25000 Explorer OL No. 31; 1:50000 Landranger No. 91.
How to get there:	From the A66 north of Appleby, side roads via Long Marton or Kirkby Thore
Start/Finish Point:	Blencarn grid reference NY 6380 3125
Terrain:	Moorland slopes with a high plateau top; some scree and boulders. Green pastures at the end of the day. Note: in misty weather conditions, map reading and compass skills needed on high level section.

The Walk

Walk to the south-east corner of the village of Blencarn and take the sign-posted bridleway route to Cross Fell. The way leads through a channel of open terrain dotted with gorse bushes and passes the farmhouse of Wythwaite. Accompany Littledale Beck by means of a grassy track and ascend the slopes of Grumply Hill. The narrow route turns north and rises steeply beyond Wildboar Scar; it maintains a north-easterly bearing, gradually climbing past a number of small marker cairns to reach the col at Tees Head, 2,532 ft (772m).

During the ascent, there is the likelihood that fell ponies will be sighted, possibly, descendants of the sturdy animals which formerly carried heavy loads across these wild fells.

The depression between Cross Fell and Little Dun Fell is the gathering ground for the headwaters of the Tees following to the east and Crowdundle Beck which runs west to join the Eden.

Bear left and join the Pennine Way, where the usual peaty conditions underfoot have been eased by a pathway of stone slabs gleaned from redundant Pennine mills. Ascend to a tall cairn and then continue along firm ground across a wide plateau to reach the summit of Cross Fell, 2,930ft (893m). The immediate surroundings contain a cross-wall shelter, an OS survey column and a litter of stone cairns.

On a clear day the effort is well worthwhile; for its wide top is an excellent viewpoint, ranging from the superb panorama of Lakeland mountains to the distant hills of southern Scotland.

However, Cross Fell, or as it was originally named, Friends Fell, has a nasty trick up its sleeve. The area has long been known as the mixing cauldron for the Helm Wind. The visible sign appears in the form of a long mass of cloud, 'The Helm', resting above the western edge of the escarpment. An easterly airstream ascends the gradual slope of the Pennines to Cross Fell where it is cooled. Because the air in the valley below is warmer, the cold wind rushes violently down the western slopes with a loud roaring noise. Fellside villages feel the full force of the blast, and the farmers fear its destructive, sudden gusts, particularly in spring time.

From the trig point, S 2979, proceed on a north-north-west bearing and descend through the encircling collar of scree and boulders to reach the spring of Crossfell Well. Continue in the same direction to meet a cairned path. Pennine Way walkers bound for Garrigill turn right and pass a building marked on the map as Greg's Hut. However, the path to Kirkland and Blencarn is to the west.

This route is an ancient way across the hills; it was a corpse road over which the dead were carried from Garrigill for burial at Kirkland. It crosses a peaty plateau on the northern shoulder of Cross Fell and leads the walker quickly down the Stoop Band slopes. The immediate area contains old mine workings where a thin seam of coal was exploited. An excellently graded track swings left below High Cap, proceeds above Cocklock Scar, then continues downhill to cross the stream issuing from Kirkdale and accompanies the main beck down the valley.

Just prior to the village of Kirkland, a footpath sign on the left proclaims a very grand-sounding title: The Hanging Walls of Mark Anthony. Follow the right of way for a short walk across a couple of fields to Ranbeck, where it would be courteous to ask permission from the farmer to view the site. Don't be too disappointed for, despite the romantic sounding name, it has nothing to do with the Romans. The area around the slight rise called 'Baron's Hill', particularly on the southern side, has fine examples of cultivation terraces. They constitute remarkable evidence of an ancient farming heritage which may date from the Iron Age to Medieval Times. After constant ploughing, even on gentle slopes, the soil would gradually creep down forming terraced banks or lynchets; it is quite likely that the area above the terraces would have contained a small settlement of huts.

Return to the footpath sign by the main track.

Kirkland is a relatively remote village at the end of two country lanes; its scattered dwellings are backed by the long sweep of the rising fells. The peaceful church of St Lawrence has medieval masonry but a great deal has

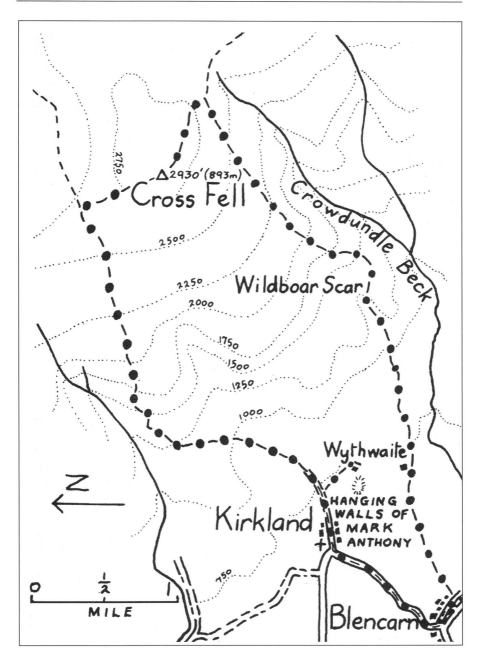

been influenced by the rebuilding of 1880. There is a thirteenth-century effigy of a Knight and a churchyard cross over 8ft (2.5m) high.

The village of Blencarn lies a comfortable mile away down a lane, where a convenient seat on the Green awaits for the weary.

Townhead and The Maiden Way

Route: Townhead, Ardale Beck, Ladslack Hill, Meg's Cairn, Stony
                      Rigg, Green Fell, Iron Well, Kirkland, Townhead

Distance: 10¼ miles (16.4km) circular walk

Highest Elevation: Curricks, Skirwith Fell 2,575ft (785m)

Total ascent: 1,929ft (588m)

Maps: 1:25000 Explorer OL No. 31; 1:50000 Landranger No. 91.

How to get there: A66 then B6412 to Langwathby or, A686 Penrith to Alston
                      Road. Just north of Langwathby take a side road to Ousby and
                      Townhead

Start/finish point: Townhead grid reference NY 635 340

Terrain: Moorland trackways and a bleak, stony undulating plateau

The great military road, the second Iter from York to Carlisle over Stainmore,
was crossed by another road running north-south called the Maiden Way.
This road starts in Lancashire, passes through the Lune Gorge, where there is
a camp at Low Borrowbridge, and continues over Crosby Ravensworth Fell
to the fort at Kirkby Thore. This road probably takes its name from Mai-dun,
the great ridge, having been raised two or three feet above ground level.
From here it climbs the western escarpment of the bleak Pennines, and runs
down to the lovely valley of the River South Tyne to Birdoswald on
Hadrian's Wall, and then northwards to the Roman camp at Bewcastle. On
its journey it passes Whitley Castle in Northumberland close to the borders
of Cumbria. The rhomboid-shaped enclosure is surrounded by a spectacular
system of defences. On the south-west side there are as many as seven
ditches with steep earthen banks. The gradients of this isolated route would
make it impossible for wheeled traffic; rising as it does to 2,192ft (668m) but
gangs of packhorses probably carried panniers of lead and silver from mines
in the Alston district along its route. It is likely that at some stage the packhorse trains would be protected by the Second Cohort of Nervii from the
Lower Rhine garrisoned at Whitley Castle.

Sections of this ancient track across the high Pennine moors are traceable
with examples of terraceways and aggers. On Melmerby Fell, beyond Meg's
Cairn, NY 657 374, the Roman road is visible in the form of a fine agger, 2ft to
3ft (0.6m to 0.9m) high, and 21ft (6.3m) wide, with large stones at the sides,
at a point where the track reaches its highest altitude. Approaching from the
south, the Maiden Way crosses Ardale Side beyond Ladslack Hill.

Nothing is known about Meg's Cairn, for this weather-beaten heap of

Meg's Cairn, Melmerby Fell

angular stones is probably an ancient burial site dating back to the Bronze Age. However, by local tradition, it may well be the work of the same tooth-less old hag that changed people to stone, and seen today in the form of Long Meg and her Daughters – a Neolithic to Early Bronze Age stone circle in the farmlands near Little Salkeld.

Judging by the mass of stones littering the vicinity of the cairn, there's been a good number of travellers petrified here over the centuries! Another interesting point on the subject. If a straight line is drawn west on the map it appears that the two sites are virtually level with each other.

The Walk

From the hamlet of Townhead, take the left-hand fork in the track to the point where it crosses over Ardale Beck. In front, and slightly to the right, stands a magnificent stone-built limekiln.

Proceed straight on uphill following the old tramway, where the route imperceptibly joins the Roman road below Man at Edge, and then continues to climb the grassy slopes to the east of Muska Hill. Below to the west lies the deep valley of Ousbydale, its far slopes rising steeply to the doleritic craggy slopes of Cuns Fell. From this point, a clearly defined delightful path ascends gradually to meet the rock-rimmed escarpment at Meg's Cairn.

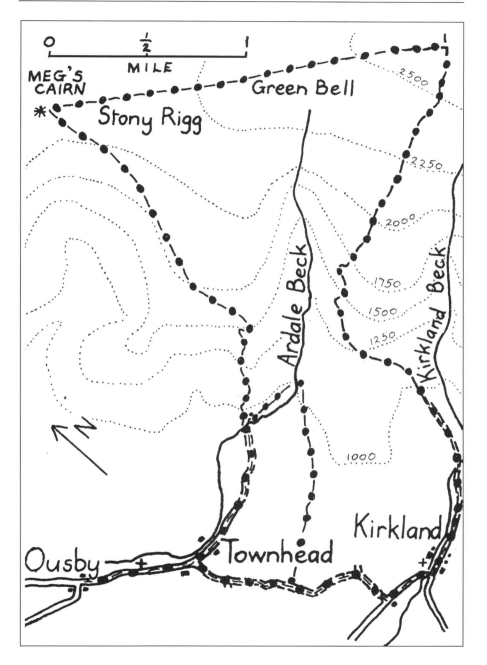

The views westward on a clear day from the plateau edge are supremely expansive. In the farmlands below and beyond the skirts of the hill slopes, there is a patchwork quilt of colours, dark green, emerald, brown, sage, yellow; all shades gradually merging away to the far horizon of purpled Lakeland peaks.

Distance gives these familiar and much-loved mountains a touch of unreality, as they stand out in sharp relief in the crisp light of the setting sun. Drifting clouds occasionally obscure the backcloth of slopes, peaks and ridges, as though to tantalise the watcher, who patiently waits for the mists to pass on and once more reveal the well-known mountain forms.

A sudden sharp breeze momentarily jerks the clumps of tough bent grass into life. The light is fading; a chillness descends; the setting sun bathes Meg's Cairn in a glowing unreal light. All around the angular grey stones appear to grow in stature; it is time to go and leave this place. Across the barren wilderness of Stony Rigg, the bulk of Cross Fell broods sullenly across the southern skyline.

From Meg's Cairn take a compass reading and walk on a bearing of 130°, an almost south-easterly direction. The walk across Stony Rigg and Green Fell is fairly rough going over a bleak, stony undulating plateau of thin vegetation, boulders and rocky hollows. The gradient rises gently throughout the journey and eventually meets the line of the corpse road from Garrigill to Kirkland; in fact, close to the point where the Pennine Way descends from Cross Fell.

Bear right and follow the route across a peaty plateau, and descend the fell slopes passing an area of old mine workings where a thin seam of coal was exploited. A little further to the north, close by Ardale Head, a bed of ironstone was worked by the Lindal and Ousby Mining Company. The ore was brown haematite, a deposit fairly rich in quality.

The well-graded track now swings below High Cap and across the slopes above Cocklock Scar, and continues downhill to ford the stream issuing from Kirkdale. Proceed straight ahead into the hamlet of Kirkland and turn right to cross over Kirkland Beck. Walk for a short distance along the road to a building called Flosh and turn right along a track. From this point, there is a pleasant one and a quarter mile stroll through quiet farming country back to the starting point at Townhead.

Ousby & Ardale Beck

Route: Ousby, East End, St Luke's Church, Townhead, Ardale Beck, Bank Wood, Townhead, Ousby

Distance: 4 miles (6.4km) circular walk

Highest Elevation: Maiden Way 1033ft (315m)

Total ascent: 344ft (105m)

Maps: 1:25000 Explorer OL No. 31; 1:50000 Landranger No. 91.

How to get there: as per Townhead – Meg's Cairn Walk

Start/finish point: Ousby grid reference NY 6275 3465

Terrain: A low-level easy walk, tracks and field paths

Early records suggest that the name of Ousby is derived from Uluesbi 1195, Ulvesbi 1214 – Ulf's by, the settlement or homestead of Ulf. The village is situated on the west side of Sunnygill Beck, named after the Norwegian St Sunivra, which appears in the Wetheral Priory records in the mid-thirteenth century as 'Sunnivegile'.

The village today, on the surface may have little to commend it historically, as its only obvious claim to fame is a camping and caravan site. However, do not dismiss plain, undistinguished Ousby, with its scattered group of houses out of hand. For, as is often to be found in small rural communities, the interest lies in the church. Dedicated to St Luke, it is to be found in quiet seclusion along the lane to Townhead, NY 635340, which eventually becomes a track to a huddle of farm buildings.

The church, a long, narrow stone building with a twin bell-cote, nestles comfortably in a green landscape backed by rising fells. Although restored in 1858, the church records indicate that its rectors have served the local scattered community since 1214.

Walking to the building on my last visit, cold spears of rain struck the face with sharp venom, as strong gusts of wind buffeted progress towards the church door. Thankfully, the building was not locked.

As soon as the door closed against the fury of the storm, peace and tranquillity reigned and the plain but homely interior was revealed. Close by the altar, lay a thirteenth or early fourteenth century rare oak carving of an almost life-size, elegant figure of a knight with crossed legs, and feet resting on a dog. Probably a crusader, his coat of mail and spurs could plainly be seen, and a short dagger hung from his belt.

The effigy was dug up from the surrounding fields some time ago and

Ousby church

placed in the church. The only other example in the country is to be found in the priory church at Pamber in Hampshire.

Sketch Map Note

Please refer to previous walk (Townhead and The Maiden Way), page 121.

The Walk

From Townhead, a track leads to the fells, past an ancient earthwork, to the secluded little valley of Ardale. At a point where the track crosses the tumbling waters of the beck, steep grassy slopes rise behind a magnificent example of an old limekiln, NY 647344. Standing in splendid isolation, with stonework and arches of Gothic proportions, the whole structure appears to be in pristine condition. Yet, there appears to be a surprising twist to the history behind the kiln.

According to local knowledge, the limekiln, constructed in 1885, was never used, never fired. If limestone, as further reported by local inhabitants, was carried by horse and cart to Salkeld Station, why wasn't the kiln used? Another interesting feature lies behind the kiln. Follow the track up the slope, and note the adjacent grassy platform that accompanies the route up the hillside. Careful inspection reveals the trackbed and rails of a defunct tramway, double track in parts, beneath a layer of turf.

This may be followed for some distance up the steep slope, and where the covering of grass can be scraped away, the rails still appear to be in quite sound condition,. But there are more unanswered questions. Did the line carry limestone down from the fellside? Was it constructed to carry ironstone from a seam below the escarpment? How long was it used, if at all? Was the initial investment worthwhile? There are probably simple explanations to these queries, but this beautifully constructed industrial building, and the mysterious tramway, remain as monuments to an enterprise that seems to have failed.

Descend the slope and return to Ardale Beck.

The broad, clear track, continues beyond the kiln, and follows Ardale Beck to the point where it has levelled out, after emerging from its steep-sided cocoon of narrowing hill slopes. Looking eastwards, unlike the craggy mountains of Lakeland, the fellsides sweep down from the skyline, like drapes of silk that subtly change in shade and texture according to the play of morning or evening light.

Cross over Ardale Beck, below the natural configurations of Cocklock Scar, to the point where the line of the Roman road, the Maiden Way, is believed to have descended Ardale Side on its way to Kirkby Thore. The right of way aims for a patch of woodland, Bank Wood, and continues past an earthwork to meet a track. Bear right and walk along to Townhead and Ousby.

Culgaith Circular: East Fellside Villages

Route: Culgaith, Newbiggin, Milburn, Crowdundle Beck, Cringle Moor, Blencarn, Cross How, Culgaith

Distance: 8¾ miles (14km) circular walk

Highest Elevation: Milburn Common 738ft (225m)

Total ascent: 426ft (130m)

Maps: 1:25000 Explorer OL Nos. 19 and 31;1:50000 Landranger No. 91.

How to get there: Turn off A66 just north of Temple Sowerby. Take B6412 road to Culgaith

Start/finish point: Culgaith, by Loaning Head Farm; grid reference NY 6125 2960

Terrain: Footpaths, field tracks and country lanes.

The place-name Culgaith contains Welsh elements, cil (corner, back) and coed (wood) – a quiet woodland corner. In 1135 it was known as Chulchet, and 1160, Culgait.

The village consists of long straggling street set well above the River Eden. The settlement developed due to the Settle Carlisle railway, but although the station is closed, trains may be caught at Langwathby three miles away.

The Walk

From Loaning Head Farm take the track on the sharp bend of the road, signposted Newbiggin Scar. From the gate and stile keep on the straight track, pass through a gate in a short section of stone wall and onto another gate and a stone stile. Bear left diagonally across a pasture aiming for a stile in a fence. There are fine unrestricted views of the eastern fellside slopes. Continue across the field to meet a stone stile in a wall then follow the hedgerow to a gate and stile and go forward alongside the hedge to another gate, a stile and a WM arrow.

Walk down a clear track with some fine oak trees to the right as the route meets Kirkandrews Wood and then curves left down to a gate and footpath sign. Turn right and descend on the road in leafy surroundings to a sandstone bridge crossing Crowdundle Beck and into the village of Newbiggin. On the left lies the church next to Newbiggin Hall.

Newbiggin; new building or house, lies away from busy main roads in a quiet rural setting. This charming village has a number of attractive cottages around a Green. One old house, Home Farm, has the date 1695 and the initials TPT. The sandstone parish church dedicated to St Edmund is distin-

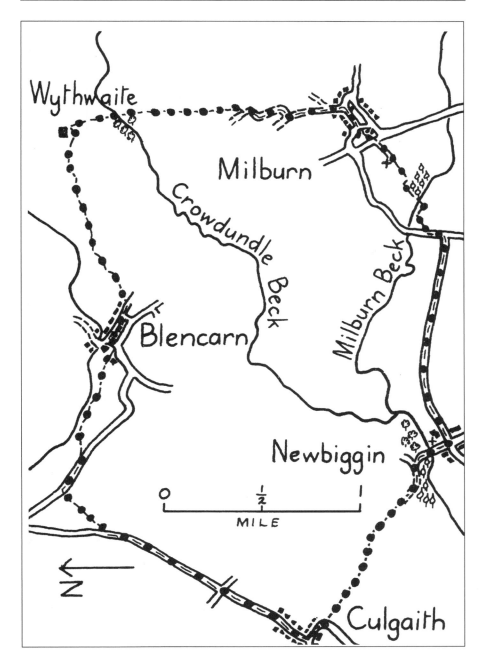

The village green, Milburn

guished by its tall slender bellcote. An earlier Norman building was repaired in 1804 and almost rebuilt in 1853-4. The east window contains fragments of fourteenth-century stained glass and the arms of the Crackenthorpe family. The church has a twelfth century communion basin and in the churchyard is a medieval sundial and the base and shaft of an ancient cross.

Christopher Crackenthorpe rebuilt the castellated mansion of Newbiggin Hall in 1533 on the site of a fourteenth-century pele tower. However, much of today's building is the result of alterations and extensions carried out in Georgian and Victorian times.

Bear left along the lane to Milburn. This peaceful route is rarely disturbed by hurrying motor vehicles and affords ample opportunity to gaze across to the heights of Cross Fell and the Dun Fells. Turn left at the road junction and gently descend to a footpath sign on the right indicating Milburn. The stile has wire netting on the top so stride over carefully. Walk ahead alongside the wall to reach a stone stile. Continue to follow the fence with the beck on the left for a short distance and look for an old boundary fence amongst the trees set at right angles. Cross Milburn Beck and follow the fence opposite on the plantation side to a stile. Walk across the field until level with the angle of a wall on the left, bear right to an electricity pole, then head left towards farm buildings and a stile between barns.

Proceed straight ahead through a complex of buildings and gates and then on down the track to cross Stank Beck. Ascend the slope to reach a church on the left.

The sandstone church of St Cuthbert, Milburn, lies in a tree-shrouded location to the south-west of the village. The present church was re-established in the twelfth century on a Celtic site, (635-687). There is a grave slab c.1300 in the porch and a Royal Coat of Arms just beyond the inner door. There are a number of examples of Norman masonry to be found: the south doorway in the west wall and in the chancel. The panelling behind the altar is seventeenth century and the bellcote of 1669 was restored in 1894.

Walk up the church track to meet the road, bear left and a WM on the right points to a small metal gate. Proceed across the meadow slanting slightly left to a gap stile in the wall. Enter an enclosed area, keep left to another small gate and WM and emerge onto the village green. You have successfully breached Milburn's defences; a much easier operation than a marauding Scot would have accomplished. It seems that Milburn has retained its original twelfth century form with the cottages and houses fitting tightly together and looking inwards to a rectangular enclosure. Narrow entrances were constructed at each corner, which could easily be defended after the cattle had been driven in for safety.

It is a most charming place and very pleasant to sit awhile in the shelter looking up towards the tall maypole which sports a weathervane. For walkers dying of thirst who haven't the luxury of a vacuum flask, the Stag Inn lies half a mile away on the road to Long Marton. As you stroll to the top end of the grassy area look back for a glimpse of the distant Lakeland hills.

Pass the school and bear left through the defences to meet a venerable NO CAMPING sign which looks Victorian; maybe Victorian campers as well as pillaging Scots were not welcome.

The way now lies along a track so take the left fork bordered with hedges. The 2½-inch OS map shows a short cut across the fields, but a WM points along the track – a precious footpath about to disappear? The track which is now walled with a copse to the left, swings right between hedges; then left, then right again to become grassy underfoot; it is interesting to ponder how the courses of these routes follow old boundary lines.

On reaching the far end of the track go through a gate and slant left to negotiate a series of wobbly stiles over fences. Continue in the same direction and aim for the far right-hand corner of a fence to a stile in the wall. The ground underfoot is now rough pasture with moor grass, bent and rush. The terrain is open, carpeted with bracken, part-dotted with thorn bushes and affords fine views of the eastern fellsides.

Look for a building in the middle distance, Wythwaite and keep an eye out for a WM on the trunk of a stocky oak tree. Follow the WM's along the bank of the beck and then descend to an ash tree. Here the arrow is pointing up the tree – a warped sense of humour on behalf of the waymarker arrow operations person.

Crowdundle Beck could be a difficult obstacle to cross in times of flood, as the extent of its catchment area encourages a vigorous flow of water. You might just wonder after all why that arrow points up the tree – a footbridge is definitely needed here. Anyhow, wade across and proceed between stunted trees to reach a gate. From this point walk through the gently rising pasture to meet a gate with the buildings of Wythwaite Farm ahead. Go towards the farm and then swing left on a grass track to a depression. Ascend the slope and continue to follow the wall across Cringle Moor. The conditions are pleasant underfoot as the way threads through gorse bushes to reveal a view of Blencarn Lake. Aim slightly right towards buildings and a footpath sign – Bridleway to Cross Fell.

Blencarn is a quiet peaceful village with sandstone built dwellings, a Green and a seat for the weary next to a young tree. At the western end of the village a footpath sign has not yet been moved from its incorrect location. Therefore, walk down the path to a stile, where you will soon discover the ancient trackway is somewhat overgrown. Approach a tied-up gate and proceed to a stile along this tree-shaded beckside route. At a point where the track bends to the right go straight ahead to pass an unsightly waste dump.

Continue across the field towards the left-hand corner to a stile in the wall. Slant up and part left across the next pasture to the left-hand corner and a stile. Walk on the same heading to reach a wall stile and on to the road. Bear right and, after a short distance, turn left at a gate with a footpath sign. Note the novel device on the chain used to fasten gates in this part of the world. Slant to the right and follow the wall to pass through three more gates. Turn left and walk for one mile along the country road into the centre of Culgaith. Turn left at the junction and back to the starting point.

Renwick: a high ridge walk over Watch Hill and Black Fell

Route: Renwick, Green Rigg, Renwick Fell, Watch Hill 1975ft (602m), Black Fell 2178ft (664m), Hartside Height, Hartside, Selah Bridge, Kiln Beck, Raven Bridge, Renwick.

Distance: 10 miles (16km) circular walk

Highest Elevation: Black Fell 2178ft (664m)

Total ascent: 1726ft (526m)

Maps: 1:25000 Explorer OL Nos. 5 and 31; 1:50000 Landranger No. 86.

How to get there: From A6 at Plumpton north of Penrith, take B6413 via Lazonby and Kirkoswald to High Bankhill, then side road to Renwick

Start/finish point: Renwick; grid reference NY 5970 4357

Terrain: Moorland slopes and grassy tops, tracks and footpaths. Some pathless sections on fells.

The place-name Renwick is either Hrafn's or Hraefn's wic, or wic on the River Raven. From the Old English hraefn, 'a raven' the name could be translated as a river with dark water. Note: The element wic frequently denotes a dairy farm or cattle farm. In 1178 it was known as Rauenwich.

The village lies at the foot of the hills with the Raven Beck flowing round the boundary of the parish. In 1341, Robert Eglesfield settled the village on Queen's College, Oxford, who as landowner kept a careful eye on its assets, such as the Mill, the surrounding woodlands and a fellside colliery.

Renwick's red sandstone houses and cottages line the street in compact groups, with some interesting barns complete with well-worn steps. Due to the unsettled Border conditions, the village was often the target for the raiding mosstroopers, so its dwellings huddle together for security as in other east fellside communities.

During the packhorse era, Renwick was one of the last outposts before the trains of ponies set out on their journey across the wild Pennine moors to the valley of the South Tyne. Accommodation and refreshments were provided for the packmen and the drovers, for there were a number of inns and alehouses that supplied their needs.

In fact, records show that the village was self-sufficient in the nineteenth century with blacksmiths, millers, a general dealer, innkeepers, miners and a tailor.

Nowadays there are no hostelries, and hungry and thirsty walkers will do

Renwick Fell

well to stock up at the Hartside Café, or save some food and drink for the return to Renwick.

All Saints Church was built in 1845 as a replacement for the former church of 1733. Its nave, chancel and bellcote were completed in the Norman style and a feature from the old church is a lovely two-decker pulpit, c.1735. Renwick, in common with nearby Croglin, also has the story of a vampire. When the old church was being rebuilt in 1733, an enormous bat flew out of the ruins and scared the villagers. One man, braver than the rest attacked it with a rowan branch and killed the creature.

The Walk

From the Townhead part of the village take the track near to the church sign-posted Outhwaite. Continue straight ahead climbing gradually on a wide track between walls. Looking back there are distant views of the Lakeland fells across the Vale of Eden. The track bends to the left, but bear right at the junction. The route continues up the slopes of Green Rigg and note the dark blob on the skyline, half right; that is the oasis of Hartside Café. Proceed to a gate, but take the gate on the left just before. At this point there is a small triangular enclosure.

Walk along the track bordered by a wall on the right-hand side and with

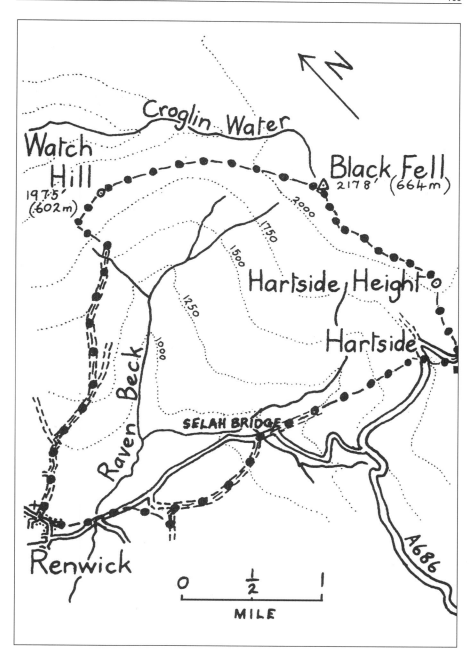

open moorland all around. Go forward to a gate and continue climbing more gently. The way is now grassy as it heads towards a gate. The boundary wall is now in a tumbled state and the ground is wetter. The wall ends and a fence takes over as you proceed to another gate, passing mine levels and tailings. The track now becomes rush-covered and overgrown. Pass the mouth of a stone-lined adit on the left; there is surface evidence that this was a coal mine. Beyond, there is a stream gully to cross, Great Stockdale Beck, with rough moorland and tussock grass predominating in the immediate area. Follow the fence to meet a fence at right angles and turn left. There is now no path on the ground; so, after an initial flog through rushes, continue up the fellside slope to a point where the fence meets a wall going right. Then follow the wall on a cushion of soft grass to the summit of Watch Hill, 1975ft (602m).

The sound of the wind and the calls of peewit and curlew pleasantly interrupt one's reveries. This sound backcloth compliments the wide views to Hartside, Fiend's Fell and the burgeoning Eden Valley. The summit of Watch Hill is decorated with a cairn and included amongst its angular pieces of stone lies a memorial tablet inscribed: I. LOWTHIAN, 1865

Continue ahead to negotiate a wall with a ruined enclosure on the far side and walk along grassy Graystone Edge in the direction of Black Fell. The way heads across well-drained open ground; a good upland tramp on a broad grassy ridge. Descend gradually to reach an area of peaty ground. Negotiate the wall and note an enclosure on the right containing a small, roofless stone building. Follow a sheep trod along a wall that becomes a boundary fence which reverts to a wall again. Beyond a gate, a fence takes over once more as the way climbs gradually. Find a route round one or two soft patches of ground and aim for gaps in the wall ahead. Pass through and bear half left to a wall running up the slope. Eventually, as a fence continues the boundary line, proceed to the O.S. Survey Column, S6373, marking the summit of Black Fell, 2178ft (664m).

Enjoy the extensive views eastwards across the rolling moorland slopes towards the head waters of the Gilderdale Burn and further on to the valley of the South Tyne. To the south rises the austere, sombre bulk of Cross Fell.

Bear right along the fence, dodging some wet areas, turn sharp left and follow the wall passing small ponds, with Hartside Café now in sight. Climb over a hurdle, ascend a little and then start to descend the slope alongside a wall. The boundary line rises almost imperceptibly to Hartside Height, 2047ft (624m). Swing right following the fence and descend the grassy slopes interspersed with peaty sections. Find a way over the fence to reach the main road at the top of the pass and go forward with quickening strides to the welcome oasis of the Hartside Café.

The café is situated on the highest part of the A686 between Alston and

Penrith. It goes into the record books as England's highest café, but it closes its doors in the winter months as Hartside is one of the cross-Pennine routes that quickly falls prey to severe weather conditions.

The A686 has taken the traveller from one environment to another in a world of landscape contrasts. From east to west the road gradually rises through scenes of wild beauty; the rippling tracts of seemingly barren upland stretch away into the distance and the cloud-shadowed clefts and valleys are coursed by shining threads of water. Here in this place, the lonely strip of tarmac is an intruder in surroundings of hued heather, rank grasses, patches of bright green moss and dark sterile peat.

At Hartside, 1892ft (577m) the transition begins: Suddenly, the road comes to life, as it tumbles, twists and turns downwards to the rich red farmlands and sylvan joys of the Eden Valley.

Suitably refreshed, walk down the old road passing an empty cottage, as the bridleway to Selah bends round to the left. The track descends steeply to cross the deep gully worn by Ricker Gill by means of an old stone bridge. The southern side of the bridge is virtually intact, but the masoned stonework on its northern side has tumbled away. This old crossing point deserves something better and quickly, before the bridge becomes too ruinous to repair. In order to preserve this unique landscape, old bridges are just as important as the remarkable stone walls that criss-cross the fells.

The surroundings are now superb as the route opens out into a pleasant valley bordered by hills. The way becomes a grassy terrace with a distant view of the Solway Firth. This delightful aspect is lost to the motorist who needs to concentrate on the numerous curves that the A686 has to offer and sees nothing but the immediate bend ahead.

Pass a lime kiln on the opposite hillside as the track swings round to reach a gate. There are limestone workings up the slope to the left as one reaches a derelict building. Its situation on this old road points to the belief that it may have been an old drover's inn at one time. Looking around there seems to be good grass available for the animals. From more recent times there is an interesting old furnace at the side of the building, complete with two large iron pans for water. The stoke-hole is clearly visible, together with a rusting iron pipe for a chimney.

Proceed through two gates and out of the paddock to another gate, then continue down the wide track to meet a minor road.

Immediately pass a newly-planted copse of trees and cross over Selah Bridge – an unusual name, possibly derived from *salh* – a sallow copse. Take the signposted public byway to the left indicating Five Lane Ends. Initially, the track has a grassy surface, which becomes a sand and stone mixture as it descends the slope; its width again points to one of the general features of an old drove road. The surface becomes grass covered again and lined with hawthorn bushes. Pass a footpath arrow on the right leading to Fellgate and also note the lovely combination of red earth and sand in the bank above the stream. Cross the stream, Kiln Beck, and go round the corner to a gate on the right. Pass under a stand of pines to meet another gate and continue down the track with a wall on the left. Cross the stream on slabs to reach a stone stile in the wall; then slant up the field partly right to a footpath sign.

Walk down the road and pass over Raven Bridge. Leave the road through a kissing gate on the right – well-endowed individuals may experience a little difficulty here. Proceed up by the fence, then slant to the left across the meadow to a corner by the wood. Go through the gate ahead and ascend to reach another gate by the farm. Continue down the road into the village of Renwick and back to the starting point.

Hilton: Wild Scordale and High Cup

Route: Hilton, Scordale, Scordale Head, Swarth Beck, Maize Beck, High Cup, Town Head, Keisley Bridge, Harbour Flatt, Murton, Hilton

Distance: 14 miles (22.4km) circular walk

Highest Elevation: Scordale Head, 1968ft (600m)

Total ascent: 1591 ft (485m)

Maps: 1:25000 Explorer OL No. 19; 1:50000 Landranger No. 91.

How to get there: M6 junction 38, B6290 to Appleby, then side road to Hilton

Start/finish point: Hilton grid reference 7350 2074

Terrain: A wild rocky dale, some bleak moorland, a deep crag-rimmed valley and pastoral ways

MOD Warcop Training area:

Telephone Range Control Officer seven days before, for details of non-firing days, Brough (017683 41661). Details of non-firing weekends in 2006: 15, 16 April; 29,30 April; 27, 28 May; 1, 2 July; 8, 9 July; 5, 6 August, 26, 27 August, 7, 8 October; 4, 5 November, 24 December to 1 January 2007.

The place-name Hilton is derived from Hill-tun; a tun on a hill; Old English. Note: the element tun originally denoted an enclosure or fence round a homestead. Later the enclosed homesteads developed into a village settlement. In 1291 it was known as Helton.

Hilton is a quiet, dale-like village situated at the foot of the Pennine fells. Sandstone-built houses and cottages line the cul-de-sac of a main street, that has grass verges and stone-cased water pumps. In the past, Hilton has risen to prominence; firstly, as the birthplace of Christopher Bainbridge, who became Bishop of Durham, then Archbishop of York, and finally, a Cardinal in Rome. Sadly, he was poisoned by one of his servants in Rome and died in 1514. Secondly, when the London Lead Company opened up the Dufton, Rundale and Scordale lead mines in 1820. Hilton quickly grew into an industrial village, changing the face of the small settlement completely. Stone buildings appeared, some cottages had an upstairs floor, and there was an overcrowding of families. The company, frequently known as the Quaker Lead Company, provided a piped water supply, bake ovens, a wash house, a school and a reading room.

Murton Fell

The Walk

Walk beyond the village limits to where the road ends, descend, and bear left on the track to reach a gate with numerous warning notices. For example: DO NOT PASS THIS POINT WHEN THE RED FLAG IS FLYING. So, either make very sure that it is a non-firing day, or that you have already checked other non-firing periods beforehand with the Range Control Officer. Also, let me reiterate the warning given before: Keep to the footpath at all times.

Walk up the track following the beck to meet a gate, and continue past the limekiln as the valley begins to narrow. A stream enters from the valley of Swindale and crosses the track. Gradually the way begins to climb above the level of Scordale Beck, with the clear entrance to an adit on the far bank. Beyond the mine level the hillside steepens considerably, with the slopes littered with stones and boulders – a riot of crags, buttresses and huge blocks of stone. To the right another stream tumbles down its rocky bed. You have now reached a stark amphitheatre of mine workings, foundations of buildings, jumbled screes, dark crags, adits and retaining walls; a veritable battleground where man and nature have met head on.

Fortunately, the commentary of an old lead miner has been recorded for posterity, and it gives a fascinating insight into his life and conditions in the mines.

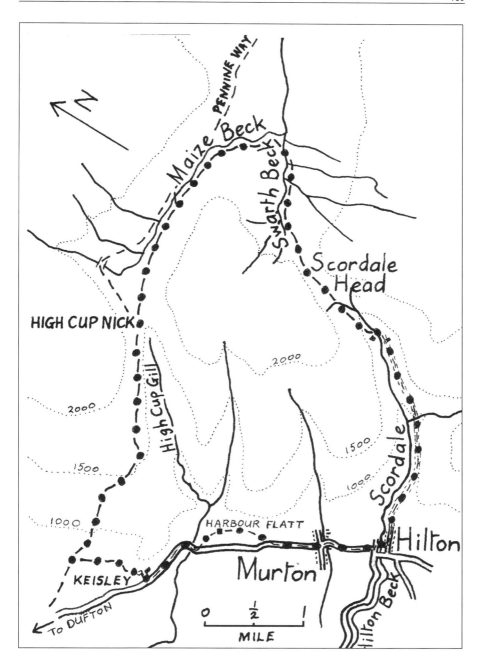

N

PENNINE WAY

Maize Beck

Swarth Beck

Scordale Head

HIGH CUP NICK

High Cup Gill

2000

2000

1500

1500

1000

1000

Scordale

HARBOUR FLATT

Hilton

KEISLEY

Murton

TO DUFTON

Hilton Beck

0   ½   1

MILE

At the Scordale Mine the horse level went in at the lowest point through a masoned arch. Mining was then carried on upwards to a flat level. Material was tipped into small trucks, and a horse pulled them along the level. Candles were placed in clay set in wall niches, and it is recorded that the horse carried an old chamber pot round its neck, with its own candle set in a lump of clay.

The mixed ore of minerals and stone was sorted, and the rest beaten with flat hammers called buckers. The next dressing was to wash the material in water on a sieve so that the heavier ore sank to form a bottom layer. The ore was then crushed and placed with water in a buddle, and the resulting slurry was moved by revolving paddles. Prior to 1880, there were two overshot waterwheels working at the mine, with a water storage pond high on the fellside. The cleaned and separated ore concentrate was taken down to the smelt mill at Hilton. The lead contained a small percentage of silver which was worth extracting; even the flue was scraped to recover any minute grains.

For years, the old miners had thrown away the loose stone, the 'cawk', as having no commercial value. After 1882, barytes and fluorspar were mined at Scordale. The barytes was found in vertical seams, sometimes reaching great depths but not more than 5ft (1.5m) in width.

In the early 1900s, two miners who stayed the week in very spartan accommodation at the mine, each carried a week's supplies in a pillowcase. The other twelve walked from Hilton and Murton and returned in the late afternoon. Their work started at 7.00am and finished at 5.30pm.

In the latter years of its life, before closure in 1952, Scordale continued to mine barytes.

Pass over a stream running through a culvert, and follow the path as it picks its way through broken ground on the left-hand side of the beck. Head fairly well to the left as the way becomes indistinct in a small depression and keep fairly high up on the slope. The ground underfoot consists of grass and rush with a small waterfall away to the right. Eventually, the line of the path becomes clearer to reach a grassy hollow. Pass a cairn on the right, cross the watercourse and walk on grass on the stream's right-hand bank. Continue on smooth grass as the valley narrows to a V-shape, with the stream now almost non-existent. Now walk on the left-hand side up the little valley, as the journey becomes a pleasant grassy way, complete with molehills – high altitude variety.

On reaching a rocky outcrop, climb up rock-cut steps and continue to ascend through grass and rush to reach the watershed of Scordale Head. Keep in a peaty groove aiming for a bouldery slope ahead. Then climb out of the peaty hollow and proceed straight ahead to reach a solitary marker stone which had been painted white at one time. This is an important guide for fixing your bearings.

Now, if any kind walker who is here on a non-firing day, just happens to have a brush and a tin of white paint in their rucksack....

Continue in the same direction to a slight depression of an emerging valley and proceed along a faint trod in the ground. There's a small bouldery slope on the right as you come to a second marker stone and a small cairn. The distance from the first marker stone is approximately 600ft (183m). In a short distance pass another stone and gently descend to a grassy depression and follow the watercourse. There's a fourth guide stone by a stony section of path, as the route crosses a small stream coming in from the left-hand side. Go forward to a mini canyon, pass another previously whitened stone, and continue on top of a rock outcrop. On the far bank of the stream down below is a small ruinous stone building. Note: the previously whitened stones mentioned in the text may originally be boundary stones, or they may be an attempt to mark the initial section of the route from Scordale Head.

Continue straight ahead to follow the small valley and keep on the right bank of the stream. As the path has now for all intents and purposes disap-peared on the ground, it's a question of either side of the meandering stream. But bear in mind that the map shows the route on the right-hand side, and in fact, a faint trod appears now and then on the right bank. However, it is as well to remember that Swarth Beck increases in width rapidly, and you will have to cross it before its confluence with Maize Beck. A number of shooting butts are passed during this part of the journey situated on either side of the beck. Cross Swarth Beck and walk past Butt No. 3, then bear left alongside Maize Beck.

The conditions under foot along the south bank of Maize Beck vary from grass to rough heather and peat, but eventually a faint path appears. As the beck levels out after its southwards course, the Pennine Way drops down to the northern bank after a moorland crossing and reaches an area of lime-stone. The Scordale Head route meets a cairn which indicates the crossing point for the Pennine Way, which now follows the southern bank of the Maize Beck. In the advent of flood conditions, Pennine Way walkers have to take the flood route, which crosses the beck by a footbridge higher up stream.

Continue to follow cairns on a clear path with pleasant grassy conditions under foot. Peeping out from the grass are shy moorland plants such as tormentil, thyme and mossy saxifrage. Suddenly, the path reaches the spec-tacular, deep crag rimmed hollow of High Cup Gill.

At the end of the Carboniferous Period great earth movements resulted in mountain building and the pushing up of the Pennine Chain. During this activity, vast quantities of molten rock entered the joints and fissures of the existing strata. This solidified as a hard, distinctive quartz dolerite rock and High Cup is a particularly famous example. This volcanic intrusion extends as an upper layer of crags round the dale head. Weathering has resulted in the formation of pinnacles and pillars standing out from the cliffs, such as Nichol's Chair. The Whin Sill is overlaid by horizontal limestone strata which is the source for numerous rivulets.

From High Cup follow the path along the north edge of the escarpment, passing Hannah's Well and across the rock ledges of Narrow Gate. The route presents no difficulty as a number of cairns indicate the way over the shoulder of the fell. The path reaches a gate and a sheepfold, and continues across grass to another gate. Follow the walled track to a barn on the right and turn down a track on the left. Pass by a barn and continue between smooth hills on a fine grassy surface. Still enclosed by walls the track bears right and meets a gate. Turn left and accompany the wall to a gate just before Town Head Farm. Continue alongside the wall to reach a gate and footpath sign. Bear to the right by the side of the farm and down the farm lane to meet the road.

Turn left along the road to Keisley Bridge, and look for the simple stile over the fence on the left. Strike up the pasture between a knoll and a copse of trees and carry on up the slope towards the farm. Go through a metal gate, bear left through another gate into the farmyard of Harbour Flatt. Turn right and walk to the end of the barn, bear left past sheep pens and across a grassy paddock to reach a gate. Proceed ahead on the lip of a grassy depression, and then down the field to a fence corner by a small watercourse. On my last visit the right of way was obstructed by a barbed wire fence, which had to be climbed in order to reach the gate. Beyond the gate, follow the fence alongside a watercourse down the field to a gate into a paddock. Carry on to another gate which leads to the road. Note: representations have been made to the footpath officer concerning the lack of helpful waymarkers through Harbour Flatt and the need for a stile.

Turn left along the road to the quiet village of Murton which, like Hilton, was once a centre for lead and barytes mining on the nearby hillsides. Continue along the by-road to reach a sharp turn, bear left and then to the right across Mill Bridge. Proceed along the lane for the short walk back to the starting point in Hilton.

Kirkoswald to Croglin

Route: Kirkoswald, Raven Beck, Low Mill, Sickergill Bridge, Renwick, Scale Houses, Clint Lane, Davygill, Lino Beck, Croglin Bridge, Croglin

Distance: 6¾ miles (10.8km) linear walk

Highest Elevation: Clint Lane 860ft (262m)

Total ascent: 630ft (192m)

Maps: 1:25000 Explorer OL No. 5; 1:50000 Landranger No. 86.

How to get there: from A6 at Plumpton north of Penrith, take B6413 via Lazonby to Kirkoswald

Starting point: Kirkoswald; grid reference NY 5560 4120

Finishing point: Croglin grid reference NY 5735 4716

Terrain: A leafy riverside way and field paths

Accommodation: see suggested list

The place-name Kirkoswald is derived from St Oswald's church. In 1167 it was known as Karcoswald, and as Kirkoswald in 1235. The village is an interesting collection of buildings, including several early eighteenth century houses. They are composed of individual designs and many are arranged with a lack of uniformity. Some houses border the street with a line of cobbles, a few stand close to the pavement and others are set at an angle behind a boundary wall with attractive gardens. One particular feature amongst its buildings is the handsome old College, which once had a pele tower.

The one main street ascends the hill slope after crossing Raven Beck and narrows to a small central square with a war memorial standing inside a railed enclosure. The Fetherston Arms in the village square is a beautiful 18th-century inn. Higher up, the street turns sharply to the right and is joined on the corner by the Potter's Bank by-road. At the foot of the village, the pretty Raven Beck continues for just a short distance before combining with the River Eden. Its vigorous flow was used to supply ample power for the village's former industries, such as the saw mill, bobbin mill, corn mill, paper mill and spinning mill. East of the village, the Raven Beck runs through a delightful valley, its pastoral course decorated by a well-wooded adornment of trees. Where the rising green pastures approach the lower fell slopes, the main stream has been strengthened by the many tributaries that drain the sprawling Pennine slopes of Renwick Fell and Black Fell.

The church of St Oswald lies to the south and is completely hidden from the village. Situated by a holy well, the building is a neat structure, with Norman and pointed arches supported on three large pillars which separate the aisle from the nave. The bases of the chancel arch display Norman mouldings which are the oldest feature in the church. The first stone church was built about 1130 and in 1523 it became collegiate, with the clergy living at the College nearby until the Dissolution. The many famous local families, such as the Dacres, the Fetherstonhaughs, the Howards and the Musgraves are commemorated in the stained glass windows. From the road a leafy canopy of lime trees line the pathway through the churchyard.

The unusual feature of St Oswald's is the entirely separate bell tower situated on the top of a nearby hill behind the church. Built in 1897, it replaced the wooden structure of 1747. Its position enabled the villagers to hear the call to worship much more easily.

The Walk

From the small square in the centre of Kirkoswald, descend a short way to a street on the left with a footpath sign. Walk past the houses, then the tarmac soon finishes and the footpath begins. Pass a leat carrying water over the river and approach a gate and kissing gate; there's a weir on the right and a pleasant riverside walk overhung with trees. Beyond another gate and kissing gate is a footpath sign indicating the way to Park Head.

The river is merrily chuckling its way through the woodland, as one passes a seat on the river bank beneath a clump of mature conifers. Ignore a private footbridge, approach a step stile over a fence and enter a meadow. Walk along the woodland fence passing a bulge in the line of trees to reach a stile in a fence – do not take the stile on the right over a footbridge.

Cross the plank over the ditch and continue along the fence to a stile. Beyond, there is a small footbridge leading to a step stile. When the route forks left proceed alongside the woodland passing through a pasture. Approach a gate and kissing gate and forward past another private footbridge. The grassy track heads through leafy surroundings, passing another access to a private footbridge and carries on through a plantation of poplars.

The route now becomes delightful progress above the river and amongst the trees. Pass a waymark and go forward to a stone step stile in a wall. As you continue along the river bank it is possible to imagine a scene from the 'Wind in the Willows', and those well-loved characters of Ratty, Mole and Toad. After a step stile in a fence, the slope on the left consists of an outcrop of rich red sandstone, the remains of an old quarry. From a step stile over a fence walk towards another stile leading over a palisade in a wall. Bear left over a small footbridge and immediately cross the bridge over the river; then walk up the track to meet the road and turn left.

At this point, the 1:25000 O.S. map indicates a right of way leading into

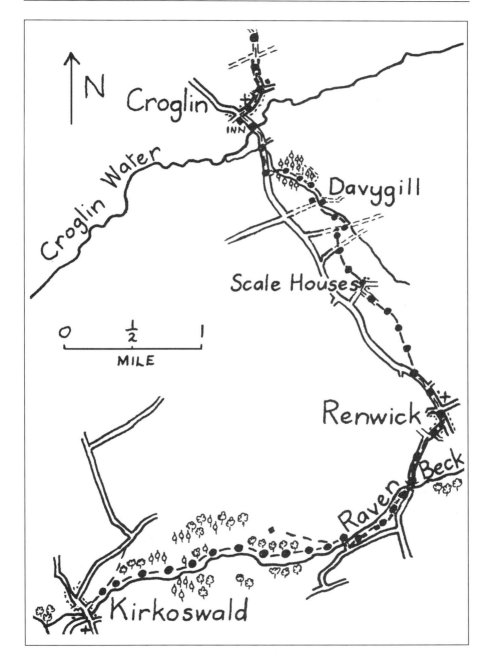

the field opposite to a house. There is no stile evident, so negotiate the wall. Proceed through the field passing below the building, a converted chapel; then keep straight on into Low Mill and exit through a metal gate. Continue to follow the river on the top side of the fence above a small meadow and reach a stone step stile in the wall. Turn left and walk along a quiet country lane passing over Sickergill Bridge. Bear right at a road junction and carry on into Renwick.

Note that the village school is now closed – an unwanted social and educational asset. This is a sad sight, just as in other places with the closure of a village shop and post office, a country pub or a rural railway line.

Turn left into the main street of this sandstone-built village and pass the Church of All Saints 1845, where the Vicar is in charge of the Benefice of Kirkoswald, Renwick and Ainstable. Walk past farm barns to a footpath sign on the right to Scale Houses. A gate leads to a trackway that gently ascends past a small outcrop of sandstone. Ignore the gate, then slant left across the small pasture to a gate in the wall and continue across the next field to a wooden palisade in the top left-hand corner. Bear left at the broken stile, walk along the wall side and a length of fence and wall to reach the corner. Pass through an incomplete stile and aim left across the field to reach a hurdle in the wall with a rickety step stile. Ascend gently in the same direction to meet a gate and turn left. Proceed down the track with a wall to the left and a fence to the right and pass through another former gateway. The track continues past farm buildings to reach a farm lane cross roads. This is the hamlet of Scale Houses.

Turn right to pass the post box in the wall and walk down the lane to a gate with a footpath sign indicating Croglin Bridge (time for hollow laughter – you will see why further on!)

Look to the right for a splendid group of lovely old barns. Walk alongside the wall to what was in the 'Middle Ages' a gate. Stretch carefully over this decrepit barrier without disturbing its molecular structure and slant slightly right across the sloping pasture to reach a gate in the wall and into the grassy lonning. The original stile in the wall seems to have been blocked. Go across to the gate on the left and aim to the right across the pasture towards the wall. [Note: what you see before you is the local version of the Roman wall. Tall, topped with wire, unclimbable. It only needs watch towers.]

No way, so retreat. Walk up the track to another gate in the wall and head across the field towards Clint Lane. There's no access to the lane on this retreat route either, nor is there a stile or a gate; so the wall has to be scaled.

Proceed up Clint Lane, pass through a gate and take the next gate on the left. Follow the wall above the beck and descend on a faint track, to the point where the beck crosses the route. According to the 1:25000 O.S. map, the right of way follows the stream; but there is no stile, so scale the wall and walk alongside the watercourse to reach an interesting double-barricaded gate. Did Hadrian have all this trouble?

Climb over the obstacle and walk towards Davygill Farm. Confusion now reigns, as the right of way as shown on the map, appears to go round the farm on its western side. However, slant to the right and make your way to a gate in the corner. Until this route is clarified you may well be advised to keep on the track and follow the wall round to the rear of the farm buildings on the eastern side.

Aim for the left-hand gate of the pair in front. Walk alongside the beck to a barbed wire fence where, according to the map, the route should go straight on. After the walls, this second line of defence against the poor foot soldiers is an artistically woven barrier backed by an impenetrable forest; where the trees are growing so closely together that they are no doubt grown for slimline matchsticks. Beat a retreat up the slope to the right, scale the tumbled wall, then bear left along the top edge of the woodland to reach a gate. Dive into the forest gloom, follow the track as it curves down to the left and then bear right continuing through the trees to reach a clearing.

Walk alongside Lino Beck to pass the secretive pheasant-rearing enclosure. Note the life-size scarecrow in modern dress standing by one of the pens. You will have gathered that this object is the third line of defence; when its eyes probably light up in an attempt to scare off the now demoralised infantry.

Cross over the stream on the simple bridge and walk up the pleasant track. Peace now reigns and the way is clear; and waiting for you by the gate is, you've guessed it, a *footpath sign*!

Turn right and walk down the road passing over Croglin Bridge and into the village of Croglin.

Later, sitting with a welcome packet of salt and vinegar crisps, the tales will be told how the common foot soldiers battled against all adversity to safely reach the bar at The Robin Hood Inn. Bed and breakfast and bar meals are available here.

Croglin to Talkin: a chilling tale

Route:	Croglin, Newbiggin Townhead, New Water, Old Water, Tarnmonath Fell, Gairs, High Hynam, Talkin Head, Talkin
Distance:	10 miles (16km) linear walk
Highest Elevation:	Tarnmonath Fell 1,263ft (385m)
Total ascent:	1,463ft (446m)
Maps:	1:25000 Explorer OL Nos.315 and 5; 1:50000 Landranger No. 86.
How to get there:	from A6 at Plumpton north of Penrith, take B6413 via Lazonby to Croglin. Bus: Carlisle-Talkin-Brampton Nos 95/95A/96. Bus Traveline tel: 0870 6082608
Starting point:	Croglin; grid reference NY 5735 4716
Finishing point:	Talkin; grid reference NY 5495 5735
Terrain:	Moorland slopes and valleys. Good fellside trackways

The place-name Croglin is probably derived from the name of a stream, with the Old English hlynn a 'torrent' as the second element. The first element may be the Middle English crok 'a bend', which is derived from Old Scandinavian krokr, In 1140 it was known as Crokelyn, in 1274 as Croclyn and in 1341 as Croglyng.

The sandstone-built houses and cottages line a quiet cul-de-sac at right angles to the secondary road, the B6413. The Robin Hood Inn lies at the junction of the two roads. This small settlement is situated at the foot of the rolling acres of Northern Pennine moorlands where the cultivated fields and lush pastures give way to rough heather-clad upland slopes.

Although a peaceful place now, there is a weird story attached to the village. In the mid-nineteenth century , a family took the tenancy of Croglin Hall and it was in one of the bedrooms that a young lady was attacked by a vampire. Because of this incident, the whole family left the area for a while for an extended holiday abroad. Some time later, when the family had returned to the Hall, the apparition reappeared. The villagers armed themselves and managed to hit it with a pistol shot, whereupon it escaped into a nearby crypt. When the vault was opened the next morning they discovered a frightfully decomposed body bearing the mark of a recent gunshot wound. The villagers drove a stake of rowan into the creature's heart and the remains were then burned to ashes.

This is a good yarn and is in keeping with the character of the area, bearing in mind the tale of the Renwick bat.

Croglin Church, 1878, is dedicated to John the Baptist; it replaced a Norman church and has a double bellcote and neo-Norman windows with zigzag arches. The church was burned by the Scots in 1346 and there is a list of rectors dating back to 1293. Opposite the church is The Old Pele, dating from the fifteenth century, which was originally the home of the rectors. The pele tower was built to withstand Scottish raids and has a tunnel-vaulted ground stage. The building has been greatly altered and the hall section appears to be of the Georgian period.

The Walk

Start by walking along the road opposite the Robin Hood Inn and keep on past the pleasant red-sandstone cottages and the church. Continue past an old quarry and turn left to ascend steeply uphill for a short distance with a plantation on the right.

Take the next turning on the right along the gravel track for a few steps and then turn left. Pass a sheepfold and continue to climb gradually across the lower slopes of Croglin Fell. The clear track affords wide views and passes through a small number of gates to reach the narrow wooded valley of Newbiggin Beck. From this point there is a choice of ways, one on either side of the valley; you can either turn right and ascend the right-hand side or bear left and descend to Newbiggin Townhead. The first route eventually becomes indistinct in a rushy area before joining the other route. The second route to Newbiggin Townhead is the clearer way on the ground and will only add on an extra half mile. This has the advantage of allowing the walker the opportunity of studying the architecture of the village inn.

Newbiggin is a quiet, charming place. There's a roadside stream of clear water with its compliement of ducks, plus a handful of red-sandstone houses and a small stone church by the bridge. For walkers using Newbiggin as their starting point there is some parking on the grass verge at Townhead.

From the bridleway sign at Townhead, go through a gate straight ahead on the left-hand side of the narrow wooded valley. The way climbs steadily up to a gate, but ignore the second track on the left that is just past a boundary stone, and pass into open moorland. The track, now pleasantly grassy, ascends to a gate in a wall; where at the appropriate season in the year the heather is in glorious bloom. Note the old limekiln to the left sitting under a low ridge.

The surrounding moors are managed for grouse shooting and you are quite likely to pass the sportspersons and helpers engaged in this activity during the season, August to October. Keep to the rights of way, bear in mind the grouse breeding season and always be aware of the effects of your presence on these wild and beautiful tracts of upland.

On the opposite hillside there is a small area of quarry workings and the

Croglin church

boundary line accompanying the track alternates between a wall and a fence. As one descends, the surroundings are very fine indeed, it is a glorious scene with billowing waves of rough grass, heather and bracken stretching away to the high moorland ridges that dominate the horizon. The route bends north and a watercourse, Eller Beck, appears on the right. Note the lonely rowan trees by the beckside.

After the withdrawal of the glacial ice from the upland regions, lichens appeared with dwarf trees, willows, birch and juniper. In warmer and wetter times birch began to colonise the higher fell slopes and, in fact, stumps of birch have been found in the peat at altitudes between 1200ft (366m) and 2000ft (610m).

From the earliest times, man and his stock began to denude and modify the landscape. The open fells were used for summer grazing, with the animals, particularly sheep, nibbling down the tree seedlings. The valleys and lower lands were extensively farmed; the woodlands and forests were greatly destroyed for charcoal and generally, due to the tremendous need for wood.

In Northern England, typical moorland develops on level hilltops or on gentle slopes and peat develops on the flatter areas or on areas of gentle slopes irrespective of the local rainfall. Areas of deep peat deposits hold a greater quantity of water and with little sand mixed in with it, the mass becomes completely saturated; it is poorly aerated, acidic in nature and usually cold.

There are three major groups of moorland: the drier heather-moor type, with the dominant plants of heather, *Calluna vulgaris*, bell heather, *Erica cinerea* and bilberry, *Vaccinium myrtillus*. This moorland frequently includes: purple-moor grass, mat-grass, heath rush, bracken, hard fern and mosses, particularly hair moss.

The bilberry moor; here the plants grow quickly to become dominant, as they tolerate both exposure and shade better than heather.

The cottongrass moor; this occurs where the peat is deeper still, even less sand and where the mass is saturated with water. Blanket bogs are to be found in the wettest parts of the moor with thick mats of bright green sphagnum moss.

The Eller Beck quickly joins the New Water and there is a view now up this wild valley which is reminiscent of the Cheviot Hills. The track is now a path through heather and bracken above the river. Note the landslip on the far bank, then descend and cross the New Water. At one time the river was bridged, but now only a single abutment remains. The bedrock makes the crossing fairly easy, particularly at a spot below the pools. Climb up the bank to regain the line of the path through the bracken where it soon becomes a faint trackway again.

The rounded hill in front goes by the splendid name of Tarnmonath Fell; this is part of the King's Forest of Geltsdale, a former royal hunting preserve. The name is an interesting one and with the nearby stream of Tarnmonath Beck, is possibly a combination of Norse and Old English elements.

Approach a gate in a fence with a sheepfold to the right. There appears to be a mixture of building styles; a stone retaining wall, two shelters, one stone roofed and one with corrugated iron. The next stage is a very pleasant grassy track as one nears the valley of the Old Water. In the distance is a shooting hut with a clearly visible rusty roof.

Cross the river via the Old Water Bridge, which has no parapets and pass a sandstone boundary stone. There are a few trees here in the valley depression that have survived due to its sheltered position. Also at this spot is a small walled reservoir with a notice warning individuals to keep livestock and domestic pets clear of the water supply. Continue up the grassy track to reach a gate and step stile. Beyond, about halfway between the stile and the shooting hut, the way cuts back to the left and ascends the fell slope. Look for a small watercourse descending the fellside, roughly opposite the last small tree and turn at that point. Looking back down to the valley there is a round sheepfold. In Northern England, particularly in Northumberland, the fold is called a stell; a stelling is a cattle fold, or sheep fold, a place where the animals shelter from the sun.

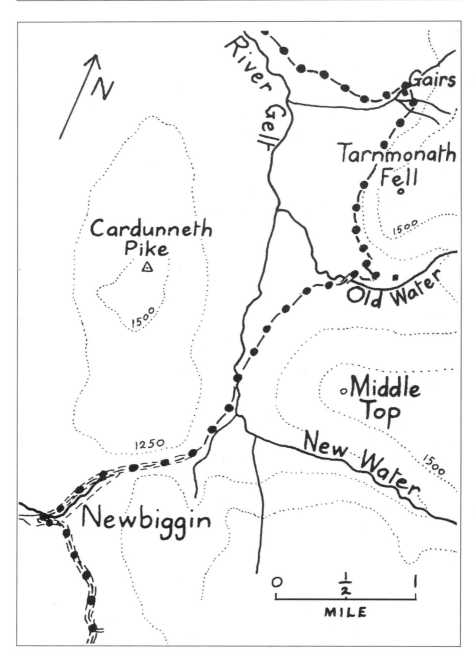

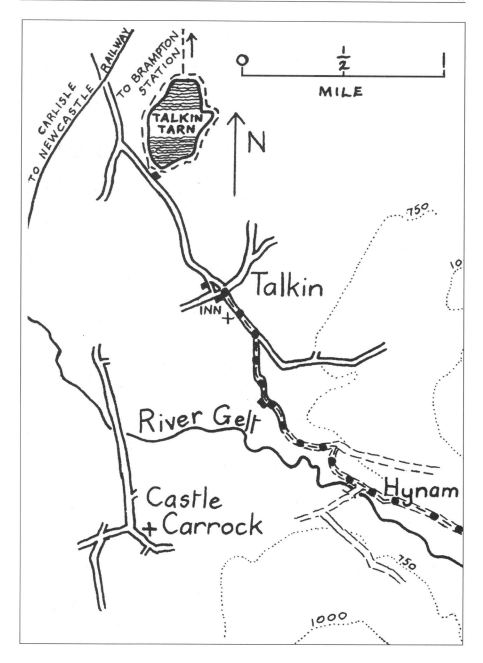

The grassy way climbs steadily and then turns to the right in a zigzag to traverse across the bracken and heather-covered hillside. Approach a gate and step stile in the fence. Ahead, clearly visible, is the impressive dipping scar on the flanks of Simmerson Hill and in the far distance there's a tantalising view of the Solway Firth. Beyond the v-shaped gap in the hills is the area crossed by the line of the Roman Wall, and the Border country called the Debateable Land.

The grass track now slowly descends, and the building called Gairs comes into view in the upper part of the valley of the How Gill. Pass some old mine workings, bear left and descend towards Gairs. This was once a substantial house but is now quickly becoming derelict; it is a shame for a building in such a lovely situation.

The track swings left and continues as a delightful grassy way to follow the rapidly deepening valley. Approach a gate and carry straight on to where the track forks. Pass an outcrop of boulders and an area of quarry workings to bear left at a wall ahead. From here the track meets a gate and circuits round the hillside high above the river. There is a wall to the right as the wide track descends an area of woodland and along the river bank. On the left, the derelict building with a rusty corrugated iron shed is High Hynam. Follow the River Gelt with its bouldery bed and deep pools, through attractive leafy surroundings. This is in great contrast to the heather-clad moorlands of the King's Forest of Geltsdale.

At this point the river has worn a channel in its rocky bed, which has also been beautifully sculptured, by the action of pebbles whirling round and round. There is a weir and a water gauging station on the far side of the impressive stone bridge; the Gelt then plunges through a gloomy rocky gorge.

Continue along the riverside, then bear right to a gate and ascend the track through woodland. Leave the path at a gate and footpath sign, bear left and walk down the track to Talkin Head. Pass the row of holiday dwellings and follow the lane to the road junction. Turn left and carry on for a short distance to the crossroads in the centre of Talkin village. There are two inns, The Blacksmith's Arms and The Hare and Hounds.

Dufton to Dunfell Hush

Route (a):   Dufton, Halsteads, Great Rundale Beck, Knock Fell, Dunfell
                        Hush, Dun Fell, Little Dun Fell, Cross Fell, Greg's Hut, Garrigill

Route (b):   Dufton, as above to Dunfell Hush, Trout Beck, Troutbeck Foot,
                        Dorthgill, Ashgill, Garrigill

How to get there: Leave A66 north end of Appleby, and side road to Dufton

Starting point: Dufton grid reference NY 6895 2505

Finishing point: Garrigill grid reference 7445 4155

Return Walking: Via Pennine Way to Dufton or, as described in the walk 'Cross
                        Fell Highest Point in the Pennines' (p115), to Kirkland and
                        Blencarn. (Map NY 62/63 no. 578 O.S.)

Return Transport: By road to Leadgate and A686 to Penrith or, by road and
                        B6277 to Alston and A686

Accommodation: See suggested list

Dufton, Dove Farm; is situated at the foot of the eastern fellsides in the Eden
Valley. Many of the red sandstone dwellings, some dating from the seventeenth to the nineteenth centuries, are grouped round a delightful
tree-fringed green. To Pennine Way walkers, Dufton is a welcome oasis after
the crossing of the bleak moorlands from Teesdale. The village contains the
Stag Inn, a post office cum shop and a Youth Hostel; there is also a car park
and toilet facilities.

On the green stands the well-known sandstone drinking fountain, a
particular magnet for photographers. The London Lead Mining Company,
which commenced mining operations in the nineteenth century in the
Dufton area benefited the village. After outbreaks of typhus and cholera in
Teesdale the company decided to spend considerable sums of money on the
provision of reservoirs and piped water supplies. They were determined to
maintain a healthy, well-housed and sober labour force.

The church of St Cuthbert stands nearly a mile away to the north of the
village. A plain building with a gallery, it was rebuilt in 1784 and restored in
1853. Its records go back to 1292 and tradition relates that it was one of the
places where Monks from Lindisfarne rested with the body of St Cuthbert, as
they fled from the depredations of the Vikings.

For such a small village, Dufton parish covers an extensive area and is
one of the largest in England. It stretches over the Pennine watershed to the
River Tees and ranges from lush pastures, woods and farmland to the vast
inhospitable heather and peaty moorlands.

River South Tyne, Garrigill

The Walk – Routes (a) and (b) to Dunfell Hush:

From the village green walk to the north-west corner, descend on the road and follow the hedged track on the right. At Coatsike Farm proceed through a gate into the farmyard and carry on to another gate. The track Hurning Lane, part of the Pennine Way, continues between tall hedges to a gate and further on meets two sets of stiles across field access tracks. A watercourse running down the centre creates a boggy section prior to two more stiles. Go forward through a gate as the track narrows with a wall to the left and a hedge to the right. The route continues between walls to reach the derelict, although characterful, farm building of Halsteads.

There is now open ground on either side of the track before it descends to cross tree-edged Great Rundale Beck. Pass through a wall stile and across the

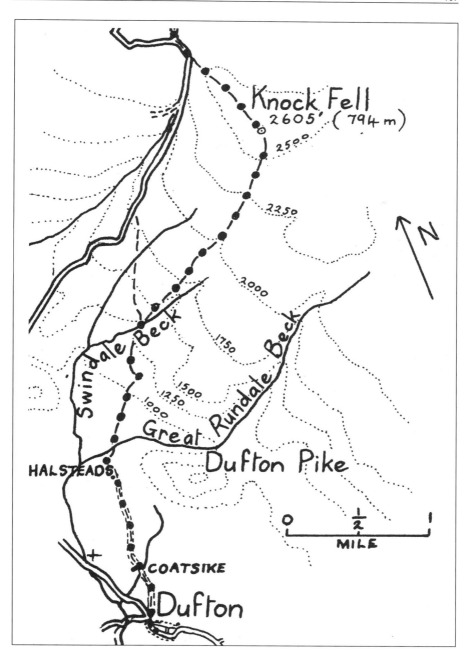

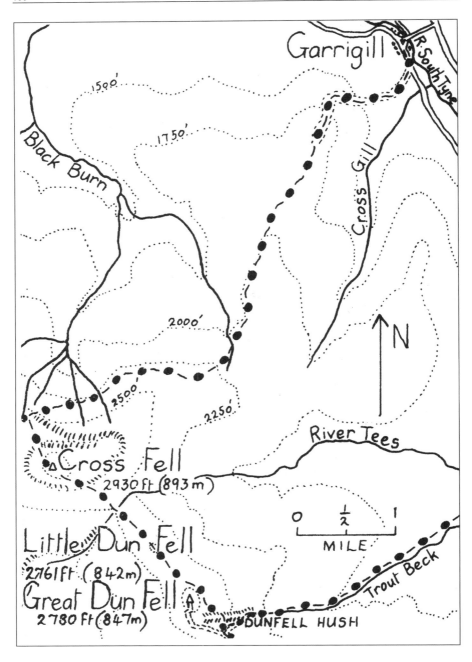

Garrigill

R. South Tyne

Black Burn

1500'

1750'

Cross Gill

2000'

N

2500'

2250'

River Tees

Cross Fell
2930 ft (893 m)

0   ½   1
MILE

Little Dun Fell
2761 ft (842 m)

Trout Beck

Great Dun Fell
2780 ft (847m)

DUNFELL HUSH

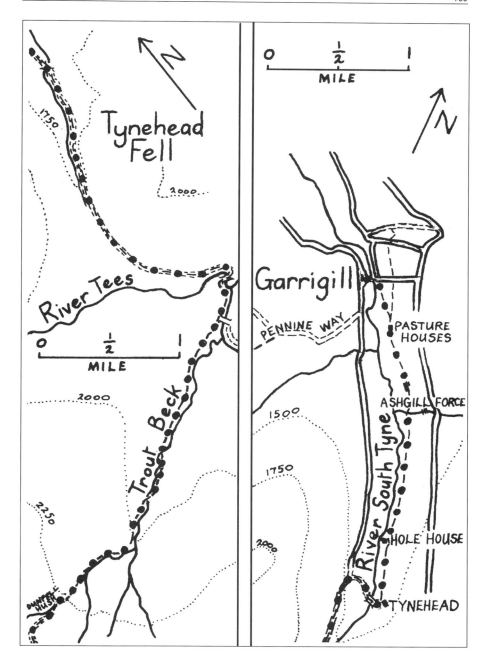

---

stream on stone slabs, with a view of the giant white sphere on Great Dun Fell. Climb gradually to a gate and a stone stile midst lovely grassy surroundings. The track swings left across a tiny stream, Small Burn and climbs up the open fell to become a pathway. Go through a wall stile, then on for a few paces to a stile over another wall and cross the footbridge over Swindale Beck.

Note: In bad weather conditions, avoiding the summit of Knock Fell, follow the wall northwards. Then continue on a path in a north-easterly direction to meet the service road to Great Dun Fell.

The scene is now a wild one, with the stream flowing rapidly over its bed littered with boulders. Climb up the steep slope, slanting to the right, and follow a cairned path along the rock covered hillside which gradually becomes a grassy way. From twin cairns, cross the stream issuing from Knock Hush and aim for the substantial cairn ahead. Negotiate some peaty sections to reach Knock Old Man, a well-built squarish structure with good views to Great Dun Fell and across the Eden Valley. From this point there is an easy walk to reach the summit cairn of Knock Fell, 2605ft (794m).

The hill slopes flow smoothly down to the farmlands below; the fields appearing as a patchwork quilt of colours: dark green, emerald, brown, sage and yellow; all the hues gradually merge at the far horizon of purpled Lakeland peaks.

From the summit cairn continue on a northerly bearing along the plateau dotted with peaty and stony sections. Descend slightly across an angular boulder field and forward through a peaty area to reach another cairn. Follow the line of metal posts in an area of shake holes to meet the Great Dun Fell service road.

Walk ahead on the road for a short distance to a Pennine Way sign and continue climbing, more or less straight on, up to the lip of Dunfell Hush.

Dunfell Hush via Cross Fell to Garrigill

Route (a):   Dufton, Halsteads, Great Rundale Beck, Knock Fell, Dunfell
                        Hush, Great Dun Fell, Little Dun Fell, Cross Fell, Greg's Hut,
                        Garrigill

Distance: 14¾ miles (23.6km) linear walk

Highest Elevation: 2930ft (893m) Cross Fell

Total ascent: from Dufton, 3251ft (991m)

Maps: 1:25000 Explorer OL Nos. 19 and 31; 1:50000 Landranger
                        Nos. 91, 86.

Terrain: The walk lies over exposed summits and escarpment slopes
                        with Cross Fell's austere bleak top rimmed by a collar of
                        boulders and scree.

The Walk – Route (a)

Cross Dunfell Hush, bear left and ascend on grass to the summit of Great Dun
Fell, 2780ft (847m), keeping on the eastern side of the 'great golf ball'. The
Civil Aviation Authority built a new radar station here in 1985 and the white
radome protects the sensitive equipment. This high altitude complex is also
a meteorological station and its instruments have recorded a wide range of
weather extremes.

Descend to a shallow depression and walk up the grassy slopes of Little
Dun Fell, 2761ft (842m). Continue in the same direction and descend to the
col at Tees Head. A pathway of rock slabs assists progress across the boggy
sections as the path climbs to a tall cairn. Proceed across the wide grassy
plateau to the summit of Cross Fell, 2930ft (893m). Here, there is a cross-wall
shelter, an OS survey column S2979 and a litter of cairns.

Descend stony slopes on a bearing just west of north to reach a cairned
path. Turn right to pass Greg's Hut, once a lodging shop at the lead mine, and
follow the clear track down to the village of Garrigill.

Dunfell Hush via Trout Beck to Garrigill

Route (b):   Dufton, Dunfell Hush, Trout Beck, Troutbeck Foot, Dorthgill, Ashgill, Garrigill

Distance: 15 miles (24km) linear walk

Highest Elevation: 2605ft (794m) Knock Fell

Total ascent: from Dufton, 2415ft (736m)

Maps: 1:25000 Explorer OL Nos. 19 and 31; 1:50000 Landranger Nos. 91, 86.

Terrain: Exposed hill summits, remote high moorland, grassy, some peat and boulders. Pleasant valley pasture (The Ravenber route).

The Walk – Route (b)

On the lip of Dunfell Hush turn right at a cairn and notice a glimpse of Cow Green Reservoir in the distance.

Early exploration of ground for mineral veins, particularly lead, meant that the method of hushing was used. On a steep hillside a dam was made to hold back water and when ready the water was released. The powerful flow tore away the ground material of soil, peat, vegetation and rock. The debris was examined for signs of ore at the foot of the slope as well as in the sides of the hush. These hushes can often be seen in the former lead mining areas of the northern Pennines.

Follow the direction of this impressive looking trench, through an area of old spoil heaps. The initial mile of descent from Dunfell Hush is on an easterly bearing and then the beck is followed on a north-easterly bearing. At first the path is indistinct on the ground, but walk on the left-hand side of the watercourse and then cross over to the other side. The beck quickly gathers strength from the numerous small tributaries as the surrounding moorland stretches away into the distance.

There are one or two deep pools now, as you cross over the left-hand side and follow a lovely grassy section. Negotiate some boulders as the way becomes a rough path clinging to the stream bank. In an area of mine workings, look for an almost hidden entrance to a mine adit just after an elongated spoil heap. The path continues to follow the north bank of Trout Beck and meets a track going off to the right across a bridge to Moor House. A little further on, the mature stream joins the River Tees at Troutbeck Foot.

The Moor House National Nature Reserve covers nearly 4,000 hectares of moorland. It is a vast area of blanket peat mosses, heather, bilberry, rough grasses and countless rivulets and watercourses extending from the Dun

Fells to the River Tees. The peaty, ill-drained moorland contains areas where water is stagnant; this produces the vivid green sphagnum moss which creates dangerous patches of bog. Nevertheless, there are many little corners where specialised moorland plants can survive: starry saxifrage, bird's eye primrose, tormentil, grass of Parnassus, cloudberry and cranberry. Look for the shy clumps of mountain pansy growing on overgrown spoil heaps.

Moor House Nature Reserve became the first British Biosphere Reserve in 1975. Research has been directed to the study of peat, its growth and erosion, the study of mosses, liverworts and lichens, moorland management, the effects of sheep grazing, biology of plants and animals, tree establishment and climate.

Cross the bridge over the River Tees, bear left and walk up the track to an area of mine workings. The tiny stream coming in from the right is the infant River South Tyne; it is fascinating to ponder on the fact that the area is the birthplace of two famous rivers. The track, which varies from tarmac to gravel is accompanied by the rapidly maturing stream.

The valley gradually deepens and various tracks lead off to old mine workings. Pass some rock outcrops and descend to cross the River South Tyne with a small gorge on the left. The farm buildings on the right are storage areas for animal fodder. Continue along the track to a cattle grid, with the sight of greener pastures beyond a ragged line of wind-blasted conifers. Pass another cattle grid and the derelict building of Dorthgill and then an old limekiln, before meeting the country lane that continues into Garrigill.

Turn right and descend the hillside track, which has both metalled and loose sections. Go through two gates and pass the ruined building of Dorthgillfoot. Cross the wooden bridge over the bouldery river bed, with derelict mine workings up stream along the river bank. Ahead lies Tynehead Farm.

Cross over the cattle grid to a footpath sign on the left, which indicates a public by-road to Yad Moss and its ski tows, as well as the path down the valley to Ashgill. Bear left and walk across the field to a gap in a wall with an arrow marker. Carry on to a gate, noting the small gorge that has been cut by the river; its bed a mixture of small boulders and bare rock.

About a quarter of a mile downstream from Tynehead there is a raised rectangular area believed to be a Roman camp, Chesters. The right of way passes through the site, with the old shafts and debris from the washing process lying between the path and the river. It is thought the Romans and their slave labour worked the alluvial gravel for lead ore which had a high silver content. In fact, the silver-rich ore was probably washed down the burn from the Clargill Head veins. These veins were later worked by the

London Lead Company and yielded upwards of 43oz. (20,640 grains) of silver per ton of lead.

Keep to the right of Hole House Farm and proceed through a gap in a fence; passing more mine tips on the right. Walk across a very pleasant river-side pasture to a stile and descend to cross a stream to a stile in a wall. Just beyond, a footbridge on the left carries a path to Over Lee House. The track along the river bank passes through delightful surroundings of parkland quality to reach the footbridge over Ash Gill. A short detour to Ashgill Force is recommended and a path leads to a wooded ravine where the water tumbles and cascades over rock steps.

Return from the waterfall; take the path that ascends the slope, and accompany the wall to Ashgillside Farm. From here, a clear well-marked route with good stiles, continues through pastures and by the farmsteads of Pasture Houses and Ford. From the latter building, take the right of way that slants down towards the river and onto Garrigill Bridge. Turn left into the centre of Garrigill.

Note: After an accommodation stop at Garrigill, the circuit of Cross Fell may be reversed by returning via the Pennine way, Greg's Hut and Kirkland, or via the Pennine Way, Cross Fell and the Dun Fells to Dufton.

Section 5: North Eden

After its journey from the extensive area of moorlands known as The King's Forest of Geltsdale, the vigorous River Gelt plunges down a beautiful well-wooded gorge. Here, centuries ago, detachments of Roman soldiers worked to quarry stone for Hadrian's Wall. The Written Rock of Gelt, as it is called, records the activities of one of these squads from the 2nd Legion Augusta. Despite the time-weathered appearance of the inscriptions it is exciting to study this evidence left by visitors to our land so long ago

Finally, the Eden leaves the high hills, woodlands and rich farmlands behind to pass by the City of Carlisle. Beyond the urban fringe, it wriggles briefly through open countryside once more, to reach the tidal waters and sandy wastes of Solway. The walking route follows the line of the Cumbria Coast Path as far as Burgh-by-Sands, with a detour to the Edward I Monument. There are wooded river banksides, quiet villages and the interest in tracing the course of Hadrian's Wall. The village of Burgh-by-Sands has a surprise or two in store.

The area of Comb Crag by the River Irthing was a freestone quarry extensively worked by the Romans. The soldiers have left their names on the rock face, and amongst those that may be seen are: Securus, Justus, Julius and Mathrianus.

Cumbria's northern border with Scotland stretches from the salt-marsh, sandy estuaries of the Eden and the Esk to Liddesdale and along the Kershope Burn to meet Northumberland. This is the 'Debateable Land' on the border, and the dispute over its ownership lasted over a considerable period of time. In the fifteenth and sixteenth centuries the area was plagued with skirmishes, raids and bloody reprisals. These events culminated in the Battle of Solway Moss in 1542, when a force under the command of Sir Thomas Dacre defeated a large Scottish army. Looking at a map today you will note that the border leaves the Esk and heads due west to meet the River Sark.

Fortified houses and farms are frequently to be found in northern England, particularly in Cumbria and Northumberland. During unsettled and dangerous times many pele towers and bastle houses were built to withstand short sieges. On the eastern side of the Eden Valley, there is a fine bastle house in the village of Glassonby (see pages 81/82).

Linear Walk 1: Talkin to Brampton Station

Route: Talkin, Talkin Tarn, Tarn Wood, Brampton Station

Distance: 2¼-2¾ miles (3.6-4.4km)

Highest Elevation: Tarn End Hotel 426ft (130m)

Total ascent: 39ft (12m)

Maps: 1:25000 Explorer No. 315; 1:50 000 Landranger No. 86.

How to get there: A69 Carlisle to Brampton, then B6413 and side road to Talkin.
                       Train: British Rail Information Tel: 0845 7484950.
                       Note: Brampton Station (Carlisle to Newcastle-upon-Tyne line)
                       lies 2 miles (3.2km), by road, south-east of Brampton Town.

The place-name Talkin may contain the Welsh tal, meaning front, forehead or end. The second element is not clear. In 1200 it was known as Talcan and in 1294 as Talkaneterne.

From the centre of Talkin continue straight ahead on the road for ¾ mile (1.2km) until the Tarn End Hotel is reached. From the far side of the hotel, take the short stretch of path down to the tarn side. There is a path round the whole shore line, but it only means an extra half mile if you turn right. The walk is a pleasant journey through the Country Park, a scenic interlude of water, woods and fields. On reaching the north end of the tarn, take the path through Tarn Wood behind the boathouses to meet a gate. Proceed across the fields to reach a road. Turn right, and follow the road for a short distance to Brampton Station.

Linear walk 2: Talkin to Brampton Town

Route: Talkin, Talkin Tarn, Tarn Wood, Wreay, Brampton Town

Distance: 3½ miles (5.6km)

Highest Elevation: Wood's Hill 384ft (117m)

Total ascent: 82ft (25m)

Maps: As for linear walk 1, plus 1:25000 Explorer OL No. 315

How to get there: As for linear walk 1
                       Bus: Carlisle to Newcastle-upon-Tyne, No. 685
                       Bus: Carlisle-Talkin-Brampton, Nos. 95/95A/96
                       Bus information line: 0870 6082608

Take the same route by Talkin Tarn and Tarn Wood, as in the preceding

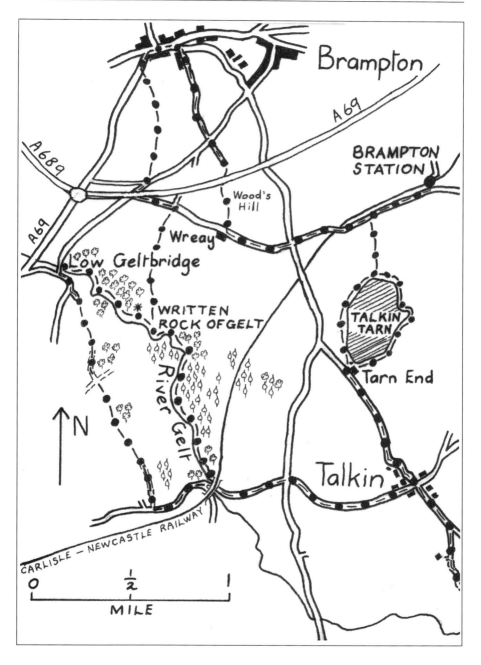

walk, to reach the road and turn left. Walk to the minor crossroads and continue straight ahead to reach the building called Wreay. Bear right and carry on along the footpath which passes to the west of Wood's Hill and brings you to Aaron's Town. Proceed straight ahead to the crossroads and keep straight on downhill to reach the centre of Brampton.

Linear walk 3:
Talkin to Brampton via Gelt Woods

Route: Talkin, Middle Gelt Bridge, Gelt Woods, Elmfield, Brampton

Distance: 4¼ miles (6.8km)

Highest Elevation: Gelt Woods 335ft (102m)

Total ascent: 72ft (22m)

Maps: As for linear walk 2 plus 1:25000 Explorer No. 315

How to get there: As for linear walk 1
                        Buses: As for linear walk 2

Bear left at the crossroads in Talkin village, walk past Chapel House to meet another crossroads and continue straight ahead downhill to pass under the railway bridge. Don't cross over Middle Gelt Bridge, but take the path on the north side of the river. Follow the river through Gelt Woods for 1¼ miles (2.0km). Just past the acutely sharp bend in the river, take the path slanting up to the right through the trees which becomes a trackway. Keep on along this route to approach the A69, and turn left along a cycle route, before turning right beneath the main road. Proceed for a little way to reach a road, and bear right to reach a footpath on the left. Follow the path as it descends through fields to meet the road at Elmfield. Turn right and walk the short distance into the centre of Brampton.

Note: As well as the circular route on page 159, there is the option of a circular walk from Talkin. Route: Talkin, Talkin Tarn, Wreay, Wood's Hill, Brampton, Gelt Woods, Talkin. Distance: 8 miles (12.8km).

The Written Rock of Gelt

Route: Low Gelt Bridge, River Gelt, Gelt Woods, Middle Gelt Bridge, Tootop Woods, Long Wood, Low Gelt Bridge

Distance: 4 miles (8.4km) circular walk

Highest Elevation: Long Wood 459ft (140m)

Total ascent: 262ft (80m)

Maps: 1:25000 Explorer No. 315; 1:50000 Landranger No. 86.

Important Note: For sketch map, please refer to page 167

How to get there: Turn off the A69 south-west of Brampton. Take minor road to Low Gelt Bridge.

Start/finish point: Low Gelt Bridge; grid reference NY 5195 5917

Terrain: riverside, woodland and pleasant undulating farmland

The River Gelt emerges from the north-west Pennine hills fed by numerous tiny streams that drain the heights of Cold Fell, Great Blacklaw Hill, Crookburn Pike and Croglin Fell.

Collectively, they form part of a sprawling upland area with a most impressive name – The King's Forest of Geltsdale. The gathering streams feed two main watercourses, Old Water and New Water, which flow past emerging limestone strata with its swallow holes and shake holes, before joining forces below Binney Bank to form the River Gelt. The vigorous river plunges down a twisting well-wooded gorge and then continues placidly on its final short journey to meet the River Irthing.

Quarries used by the Roman army are well-recorded to the south of Hadrian's Wall, where legionary detachments working these sites frequently carved inscriptions and the names of their officers on the rock faces. The area of Coombe Crag, NY 591 650, was a freestone quarry extensively worked by the Romans. The soldiers have left inscriptions on the face of the rock, amongst which may be seen the names Securus, Justus, Julius and Mathrianus.

The Written Rock of Gelt, 1½ miles (2.4km) south of Brampton is one of the major examples and records the activities of a vexillation of the 2nd Legion Augusta.

The Walk

There is a small parking area by Low Gelt Bridge. Close by are two notice boards, one proclaiming Lower Gelt Wood R.S.P.B. Reserve and the other stating Brampton Angling Association – Private Fishing Only.

c(enturia Iul(i) Peculiaris vexil(l)atio
leg(ionis) XXV(aleriae) V(ictricis)

ΛΚΛ·I ECIT ·ET ΛΜΙΟ
IIVJTVS   LEGIONE·SEXS ET

VE X·L·IEG · II ΛVG OF· ΛPR   ΛPRO· T·ΛΛΛΛ·IΜΟ
SVB·ΛGRICOLΛ · OPTIONE   CONJVLIBVS
                              OFICINΛ· MERCΛTI

MERCΛTIUJ · FERNI

Hand-transcribed inscriptions from the Written Rock of Gelt

From this point a delightful riverside track wanders through mature woodland containing beech, oak, sycamore, alder and willow. In some places the
fast-flowing Gelt has worn strid-like channels in the sandstone; in other
sections, the swirling white water has bitten deeply into the soft bedrock,
using stones and pebbles to batter, gouge and scoop out circular hollows in
the rocky channel. If the resident fish have to negotiate the rushing water in
the rocky courses, they probably end up so flat-nosed and bemused, that
they simply give themselves up to the patient anglers.

After an easy level walk of ½ mile (0.8km), look for a small squared stone
on the left-hand side of the track at ground level. Here, eleven stone steps
rise to a narrow traverse beneath the sandstone cliffs and with a final
heave-up using a convenient tree growing out of the rock, the intrepid traveller comes face to face with the inscriptions. Time and weather has eroded
some of the letters making them difficult to read, but many can be deci-
phered with care and patience.

However, before you attempt to shift your footing for a better view,
remember you are now about 30ft (9.1m) above the track. Photography is
difficult but better results may be achieved with a reasonably wide-angle
lens. The trunk of a friendly tree can be used as a backrest and this extra
stability will enable you to obtain satisfactory pictures. A warning must be
given; don't step back to admire your work unless you have previously
organised the extra support of the Almighty!

When your muscles start developing the wobbles, it is prudent to retreat
down to the riverside path and make good use of the many wayside seats to
recover one's equilibrium. Now you know why this particular walk is only
four miles long.

Low Gelt Bridge

Nevertheless, despite the time-weathered state of the inscriptions, it is a great thrill to look at this fascinating evidence left by visitors to our land many centuries ago.

Half a mile further on, following the River Gelt, is a quarry inscription near ground level on the rock face of Pigeon Crag, which lies on the south side of the river, NY 5300 5785. Close by there is a small niche with a projecting altar cut into the rock.

Tennyson wrote:

The Vexillary
Hath left crag – carven o'er the streaming Gelt".

After the excitement of the Roman inscribed rocks, the visitor has the pleasant option of completing a short circular walk.

Follow the River Gelt in its lovely wooded surroundings to Middle Gelt Bridge. Cross the river bearing right past the inn, a convenient hostelry, then continue up the road for just over a quarter of a mile. Turn right along the right-hand track through Tootop Woods. Proceed by path via Long Wood, then walk past Priest's Wood to a crossroad of tracks. Keep straight on to meet the minor road just south of Low Gelt Bridge. Bear right for a return to your starting point.

Carlisle and Hadrian's Wall

Route: Carlisle Railway Station, Cathedral, Castle, Sheepmount,
                             River Eden, Grinsdale, Kirkandrews-on-Eden, Beaumont,
                             Burgh by Sands, Edward I Memorial

Distance: To Burgh by Sands, 7¼ miles (11.6km), linear walk.
                             Optional there-and-back: Burgh by Sands to Edward I
                             memorial and return, 2½ miles (4km)

Highest Elevation: Wormanby 95ft (29m)

Total ascent: 69ft (21m)

Maps: 1:25000 Explorer OL No. 315; 1:50000 Landranger No. 85.

Starting point: Carlisle Citadel Railway Station, grid reference NY 4020 5550

Finishing point: Burgh by Sands, grid reference NY 3275 5914; Edward I
                             Memorial grid reference NY 3257 6093
                             Note: Bus Traveline: 0870 6082608

Terrain: Easy walking, river bank and pastures.

The Roman name for Carlisle was Luguvallium, which means 'the wall of god Lugus'. To the old name was prefixed the Welsh work, caer, 'city'. In 1130 it was known as Caerleoil.

The Walk

Leave Carlisle's fine-looking railway station *(note the taxi rank, regarding the return from Burgh by Sands)* and walk ahead towards the two sandstone towers of the Citadel. This impressive building is the last remaining gateway of the old city defences. Proceed through the archway into English Street, cross the road by the traffic lights and pass into the pedestrianised shopping area. The Carlisle Cross stands in the middle of this open space, and in front of the Old Town Hall which houses the Tourist Information and Visitor Centre. Bear left down Castle Street. On the left stands the fine red sandstone Cathedral, although there are numbers of dark grey stones that were possibly taken from the Roman Wall. The Cathedral has a Visitor Centre, a bookshop and a restaurant.

Henry I granted a site for the foundation of a religious establishment in about 1102 for Augustinian Canons. Construction of the church began in 1130; a few years later Henry created the see of a bishop, and the Priory became a Cathedral.

The building has a fine Norman west facade, but the nave only partially survives. There were eight bays originally, but six were destroyed by the

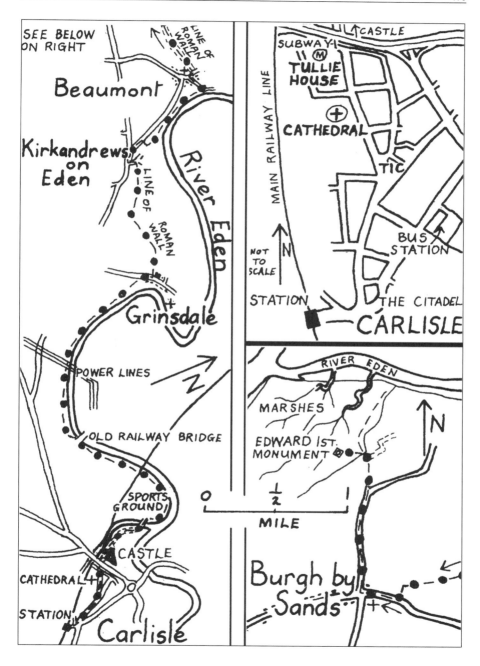

Scots between 1645 and 1652. A well-preserved and very spectacular part of the Cathedral is the chancel; the roof of which is beautifully decorated with flowing tracery.

The famous Flemish triptych which was originally housed in St Wilfrid's Church, Brougham, was restored by the Victoria and Albert Museum, and may now be seen in Carlisle Cathedral.

Continue along Castle Street to pass the excellent Tullie House, Carlisle's new Museum and Art Gallery. There you will learn the facts about Carlisle and its turbulent history. Tullie House is renowned for its unique collection of Roman artefacts.

Cross under the busy road by means of the subway to appear on the far side in front of the castle. Its magnificent Keep, well-preserved and still watchful, not against invaders, but over the continuous tide of moving traffic. Only captured once despite being attacked by Robert the Bruce and Bonnie Prince Charlie, it now houses an exhibition about its history and a museum of the King's Own Border Regiment.

Turn left and walk along to the west side of the castle. Bear right into the Devonshire Walk car park and continue to the end of the curtain walls. Then bear left down the access drive to the Sheepmount sports ground. Ahead lie a quantity of masoned stones dredged from the river, and set where the Roman bridge abutment was thought to have stood.

Turn left and cross the bridge over the Caldew, a rather off-colour looking river when compared with its early stages back of Skiddaw. Bear right and follow the trackway alongside the Caldew until its confluence with the Eden. The aspect is a very pleasant one indeed, with the playing fields on one side and the river on the other.

Pass beneath the main line railway bridge, with a red brick building and an industrial gas depot on the left. Then comes a gaggle of pylons, and the site of another old building. Cross the bridge over the small beck and walk along a railed path by the river. Continue under the old railway bridge and ascend the steps to the left to reach the line of the old railway; note the metal barrier barring the way across the river. Bear right along the old track bed passing the site of **Milecastle No. 67**. Continue straight ahead, and then slant to the right on a path and then down steps to a footbridge. Ignore the path on the left and keep alongside the fence on the river bank to reach a step stile over a fence.

Carry on past a WM to reach a small sandstone pillar with the faint impression of a cross carved into its surface. Keep straight on along the edge of the field passing a gap and a ladder stile. Pass under pylons to arrive at a step stile over a fence, descend steps, cross over a footbridge and ascend the far side. Continue along the edge of the field to a stile, descend steps, swing to the right along a gully side to cross a footbridge. Ascend steps and pass through a copse of trees. **Milecastle No. 68**.

Proceed between trees and hedge, descend steps and across planking. There's bracken and a hedge on the left with trees to the right, as you walk above the river to arrive at a step stile. Cross the meadow passing a waymarker post, and bear right following a line of trees and bushes to meet a WM and Cumbria Coast Walk sign.

Go over the footbridge, and on through the field to reach a step stile and footpath sign by the side of a farm. Turn right along the road in Grinsdale. This village, a small quiet community of farms and cottages lies at the end of a lane on a bend of the Eden. The church, St Kentigern, stands on its own overlooking the river and is accessible by footpath. It was rebuilt in 1740 after becoming ruinous.

Turn left into the farmyard at Park Farm, footpath sign to Beaumont, to a gate and stile. Proceed on a track through the pasture passing a section of neat walling and a clump of trees. **Milecastle No. 69**. The route is now following the line of the Wall. Go through a gate ahead with a WM and follow the hedge. Ignore the gates and continue along the hedgerow down to Sourmilk Bridge; there's a stile to negotiate at both ends. Carry on up the hedgeside to a stile in the fence, follow the double fence on top of a mini escarpment to a stile. Bear left as the path continues along the edge of the slope to reach a stile; a number of WM's here.

Descend to a step stile and turn left along a track to meet the road. Turn right and follow the road through Kirkandrews-on-Eden. Bear right where the road forks and continue past the telephone box and then the churchyard to reach a footpath sign and gate. Leave the road and walk along the hedge to a small gate and bear right by tennis courts. Turn left at the end of Centre Court and pass the umpire's hut and climbing frames to reach a stone step stile. Continue along the fence to a stile and footpath sign. Pass a large house to meet a stile and carry on along the top of the slope. **Milecastle No. 70**.

Turn sharp right down steps and descend to the river's edge. Promenade along the river bank, cross a footbridge and ascend to walk above the river once more. The path then becomes a pleasant leafy way above the river. This section through The Heugh has been well-engineered and well-stabilised – an extremely fine part of the Cumbria Coast Walk. There's a view through the trees down to the river, and to the Fish House situated on the far bank.

Approach a small gate leading on to the road. Turn left and walk into the village of Beaumont – the name means 'beautiful hill'. This is another quiet farming community on the banks of the Eden. The small triangular village Green supports a small tree and an enclosing seat with a plaque: THIS COMMEMORATES THE VISIT OF CLLR. JOHN AMOS, MAYOR OF

CARLISLE. SUNDAY 14th APRIL 1991. This pleasant area is surrounded by houses of varying architectural styles.

The plain small church of St Mary was built in the twelfth century on the site of a Wall Turret, No. 70a. When work was done in the churchyard, it was discovered that Hadrian's Wall at this point was 9ft (2.74m) wide. The church has served the villages of Beaumont and Kirkandrews-on-Eden since 1962.

Bear right on the lane going north, and after a short distance turn left at a footpath sign to Burgh by Sands. Regain the line of the Roman Wall and walk down a hedged track. In a field to the north is a fine example of a *tractorum knackerei*; it now stands totally immobile and wreathed in vegetation.

King Edward I monument, Solway Marshes

Keep on this route straight ahead, pass through a gate where the way forks, and head along a partly grassed track. Between Beaumont and Burgh by Sands investigations have revealed the sites of one Milecastle and three Turrets. This pleasant route is still hedged on either side with views across the fields towards the Solway Firth. Eventually, the track narrows to become a grassy pathway and reaches a step stile.

The way ahead still follows the course of the Wall, which is marked by a line of hawthorns, crab apple trees and bushes. Cows now lie contentedly where, centuries ago, Roman auxiliaries patrolled. On reaching a stile, cross over the footbridge and bear left along a hedge, you have now left the line of the Wall. Arrive at an artistically created, short metal ladder stile, and turn right. Walk up the road to reach the village of Burgh by Sands.

This linear village (pronounced 'Bruff') stretches westwards from cross-roads, and has the important rural facilities of an inn, a village hall and a shop. The church of St Michael has a broad fourteenth-century tower, and was obviously built with defence in mind. It has no doorway on the outside, and only small windows; this compares with the principle of a bastle house or pele tower, and like those structures, has a tunnel-vaulted ground floor. Another clear feature is that the church is built with stones from the Roman fort of Aballava lying astride the Wall. In fact, the church stands almost in the middle of where the Roman fort stood.

Burgh has another surprise, which is not so obvious, in the form of nearby Lamonby Farm. It was the custom in parts of the country of providing a clay-built house for a newly-wed couple. Many of these clay-walled build-ings survive in this section of the Solway Plain, although many are now incorporated in later buildings. Clay was used because it was in plentiful supply, also with frequent Border raids, these buildings were cheap to replace.

The construction of the building was simple in the extreme, providing an interesting example of the 'cruck' type of structure. The whole building was no doubt put together by unskilled labour, with the assistance, perhaps, of the local carpenter. The roof itself was thatched, and externally, the walls were coated with whitewash which, after many successive coats, formed a thick durable skin. This annual whitewashing was essential as protection against the weather.

For a final interesting thought; this type of building had an entrance for all inmates, human and animal. A resident would know the layout of the building, but a stranger may take the wrong turning and come face to face with a cow!

Optional there-and-back route from Burgh by Sands: from the crossroads in the village, turn north along the lane and proceed for a distance of three-quarters of a mile. At a point where the road bends to the north-east, proceed straight on through a gate. After the second stile, walk across the grassy saltings to the King Edward I monument. The stone pillar marks the spot, where according to local tradition, he died on July 7th 1307, while encamped, awaiting for safe tidal conditions to ford the Solway channels.

Return the same way to the village of Burgh by Sands where, no doubt, trans-port arrangements have been previously organised.

The River Irthing, Comb Crag and Wall Bowers

Route:	Chapelburn, River Irthing, Comb Crag Wood, Comb Crag and return by same route or, continue to Wall Bowers and return
Distances:	Wall Bowers to Comb Crag and return, 1 mile (1.6km) Chapelburn to Comb Crag and return, 2 miles (3.2km) Chapelburn, Comb Crag to Wall Bowers and return, 1½ miles (2.4km) *(All linear walks)*
Highest Elevation:	Wall Bowers 476ft (145m)
Total ascent:	From River Irthing to Wall Bowers 213ft (65m)
Maps:	1:25000 Explorer OL No. 315; 1:50000 Landranger No. 86.
How to get there:	A69 Carlisle to Hexham. Four miles (6.4km) east of Brampton, take side road to Low Row and Chapelburn or, side road from Brampton via Lanercost and Banks to Wall Bowers
Start/finish point:	Chapelburn grid reference NY 5985 6460 Wall Bowers grid reference NY 5905 6538
Terrain:	River bank and woodland walking

At Greenhead, on the main A69, Brampton to Hexham road, a secondary route, the B6318, begins its angular twisting route to the Liddel Water, the Border between Cumbria and Scotland. After crossing the River Irthing at Gilsland, the road climbs to pass a minor road on the left signposted to the Roman Wall and the fort of Birdoswald (CAMBOGLANNA), which means 'the crooked bend', referring to the winding course that the river takes here. This road runs along the line of the Wall on the north side of the Irthing gorge with distant views towards the wild wastes of Spadeadam. This is Cumbria's remote, sparsely populated, northern territory; wild acres of forest, upland pasture and craggy moorland outcrops; a land of tumbling streams, sparkling becks and burns.

The Walk

Just past Wall Bowers, opposite a road junction, a footpath leads south towards Comb Wood. It crosses the line of the Vallum to bear left down through a partially wooded area towards a gap in that rocky outcrop. This sharp ridge of Comb Crag shelves steeply southwards, its hard formations forcing the river to swing sharply round in a U-shaped bend. The area of Comb Crag was a freestone quarry, extensively worked by the Romans. This

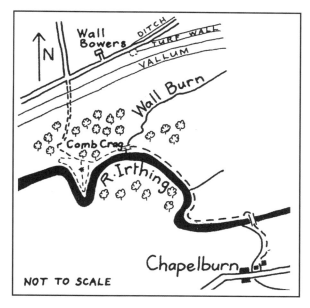

NOT TO SCALE

spot has an atmosphere all of its own. At the gap, an excellent place for an ambush, are many modern examples of the graffitic art, don't be downhearted these are not Roman inscriptions! Pass through the gap, bear right, and follow the ridge towards the river for a few yards, not along the grassy top, but on the ledge on the side to a clearly defined rock face. The inscriptions SECVRVS and IVSTVS are clearly to be seen near the foot of the rockslab, NY 591 650.

The area of Comb Crag was a freestone quarry extensively worked by the Romans. The soldiers have left inscriptions on the face of the rock including their names:

(enturia)
Securus C – AP – Iustus – 'Securus the Centurion of Ap – – – Justus'
Iulius – 'Julius'
Stadus f(ecit) – 'Stadus did this'

The location may also be approached by a longer and more interesting route from the minor road at Chapelburn on the south side of the River Irthing. Take the right of way between two buildings, descend the slope and follow the east bank of the burn passing a waterfall to reach the substantial foot-bridge over the River Irthing. Cross over and follow the river bank to a stile on the edge of the wood. The way seems to disappear here but take heart, continue through the site of a small disused quarry alongside the river now running through a delightful wooded valley area crossing Wall Burn by means of a footbridge.

In front the land rises in the form of the narrow ridge thrusting down to the river. At this point traverse to the right climbing the slope to the gap, and follow the directions as given in the previous route.

The whole area is extremely beautiful, particularly in springtime. The sunshine filtering through the emerging leaves dapples the ground with

River Irthing, Comb Crag

irregular patterns of light, the dark wooded slopes are entwined with yellow splashes of primroses, and the murmuring movement of the river provides a background lullaby of sound. This lyrical spot has an atmosphere all of its own. Just stand quietly still for a moment or two and drink in the surroundings. The whole immediate aspect of trees, flowers, running water and rock forms a perfect composition of the natural order of things. After a dark northern winter, a spring morning such as this, would most certainly have given an impetus to the soldiers of a foreign power, in their task of extracting blocks of stone to build a remarkable frontier wall those centuries ago. The inscriptions are not spectacular, but they do help to focus the mind in creating an atmosphere of timelessness in such a beautiful place.

Return by the same route to the original starting point. Or, walk from Chapelburn to Wall Bowers, or vice versa; having arranged transport to pick you up.

Dacre: a walking & sightseeing excursion

Route:	Dacre Village, Dalemain House, West Park, Flusco Hill, Dacre
Distance:	3½ miles (5.6km) circular walk
Highest Elevation:	Souland Gate 630ft (192m)
Total ascent:	292ft (89m)
Maps:	1:25000 Explorer OL No. 5; 1:50000 Landranger No. 90.
How to get there:	From A66, Penrith to Keswick
Start/finish point:	Dacre NY 460 266
Terrain:	Pasture, parkland, side road

Visitors to this north-west corner of England may care to combine their walking with a little sightseeing.

Dacre is an attractive village, quietly isolated, yet barely a mile and a half from the popular northern tip of Ullswater. The village, with its interesting church and nearby castle, is conveniently situated for a visit to Ullswater. There's an opportunity to enjoy a cruise on the lake to Howtown and then a pleasant walk along the shore line back to Patterdale.

It nestles at the foot of descending hill slopes above the banks of the stony-bedded Dacre Beck. The settlement has remained unspoilt, shyly hidden from the asphalt conveyor belt of the A66, which sadly now fears no competition from the dismantled Penrith to Cockermouth railway. From the village street, one is able to glimpse quiet peeps of the rounded hills of Great Mell Fell and Little Mell Fell, the advance guard of a greater promise beyond.

From Dacre there is also the pleasure of an easy walk to Dalemain. This historic house contains fine furniture, family portraits, ceramics and an interesting collection of toys. Look for Mrs Mouse's house on the back stairs. Visit the famous garden and enjoy the homemade teas.

Suitably refreshed, return via West Park and Flusko Hill, and then via the minor road into Dacre. Distance 3½ miles (5.6km).

It is well worth leaving the fleshpots of Pooley Bridge with its ice-creams and picture postcards to explore a triangle of countryside west of Dacre. Here one may leisurely travel along a wandering thread of country lanes past quiet hamlets and snug farmsteads, by stream bank and hill slope to Matterdale.

But don't be in a hurry to leave Dacre. The church and Castle dominate the village and provide its essential character. Fourteenth-century Dacre Castle, with its massive sandstone battlemented walls, was originally a pele tower – one of many built in the north country to protect the people of the community and their animals from the plundering raids of the border reivers. In 1723, the castle was sold to Edward Hasell of Dalemain, and it remains part of the Hasell estate. The castle is a private residence and is not open to the public.

The present church, St Andrew, stands at the probable site of the Anglo Saxon monastery mentioned in Bede. The tower is Norman, and the nave has side aisles and the arcades date from the early thirteenth century. The pillars are a mixture of round on the north side and octagonal on the south. There's a surprise waiting for you on the south side of the church. Look for the door on the south side of the church and then when located study the fascinating lock. Joined to the door is the lock and key given by Lady Anne Clifford; it bears the date 1671 and the initials A.P. for Anne Countess of Pembroke. There are two other treasures in the chancel in the form of inter-esting fragments of stone cross shafts. One is Anglian, bearing intricate vine scrollwork and a human faced beast, about 800 AD, and the other is of the Viking period; (its panels from top to bottom) its lower panel indicates Adam and Eve, with the Tree and the Serpent.

Before you leave, walk round the churchyard and look for the Dacre Bears. These are carved stone figures marking the four corners of the original graveyard. Medieval people liked a good tale, particularly ones concerning animals. The story unfolds anti-clockwise. In the NW corner the bear is asleep, with its head resting on a pillar. In the SW corner a small lynx or cat has jumped onto the bear's back. The bear's head is turned looking at the creature. In the SE corner the bear stretches his right paw over his right shoulder. In the N.E. corner, the best-preserved carving, the bear looks extremely satisfied after obviously dining on the intruder.

The castle, with its fourteenth century square pele tower has large turrets at the angles, and was altered in the seventeenth century by the insertion of square headed windows. The basement of the pele tower consists of two tunnel-vaulted chambers. One the main floor is the hall, and above that is the solar called the King's Chamber. This is connected with a vague tradition that three kings, Athelstan, Constantine and Owain, met at Dacre in 926. The castle is four hundred years later, but it may be in the immediate vicinity of where the meeting took place.

The Walk

After viewing the church, there is an access to the right of way running along the southern boundary of the churchyard. Follow the track round the perim-eter of Dacre Castle to meet a small conifer plantation. The route swings left and follows a small watercourse. Walk past a belt of mixed woodland and approach the historic mansion of Dalemain.

The track continues round the eastern side of the house and heads

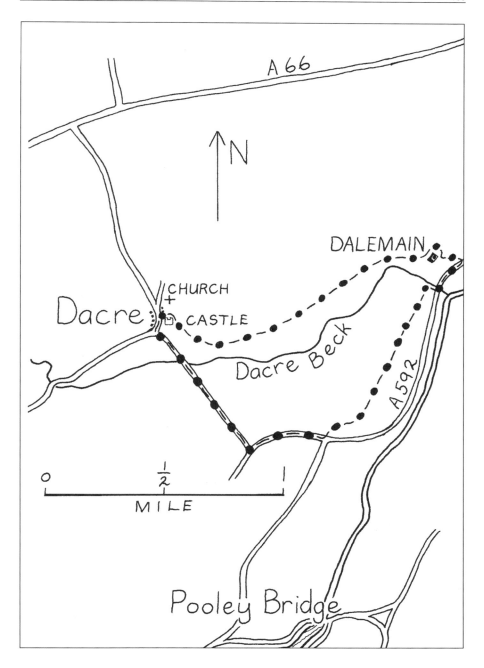

The Dacre Bear

towards the main A592. Turn right along the road for a short distance, cross Dacre Beck, and immediately turn right along the beckside path to Dacre Bridge. Turn left.

The path leads across West Park alongside Langfield Wood, and follows the boundary over the gentle swelling of Flusco Hill. Swing to the right to reach the main road. Bear right for the last stage of the walk via the minor road back into the village of Dacre.

Accommodation

Ainstable: New Crown Inn, Ainstable, Nr. Carlisle CA4 9QQ. Tel: 01768 896273

Appleby: Bongate House, Bongate, Appleby-in-Westmorland CA16 6UE. Tel: 017683 51245

Armathwaite: Dukes Head Inn, Armathwaite, Carlisle CA4 9PB. Tel: 016974 72226

Askham: Punchbowl Inn, Askham, Penrith CA10 2PF. Tel: 01931 712443

Blencowe: Little Blencowe Farm, Blencowe, Penrith CA11 0DG. Tel: 017684 83338

Bolton: Eden Grove Farmhouse, Bolton, Appleby-in-Westmorland CA16 6AX. Tel: 017683 62321

Brough: River View, Brough, Kirkby Stephen CA17 4BZ. Tel: 017683 41894

Cautley: St. Mark's Guest House, Cautley, Sedbergh LA10 5LZ. Tel: 015396 20287

Croglin: The Robin Hood Inn, Croglin, Carlisle CA4 9RZ. Tel: 01768 896227

Crosby Garrett: The Old Rectory, Crosby Garrett, Kirkby Stephen CA17 4PW. Tel: 017683 72074

Crosby Ravensworth: Wickerslack Farm, Crosby Ravensworth, Penrith CA10 3LN. Tel: 01931 71526

Culgaith: Shepherds Croft, Culgaith, Penrith CA10 1QW. Tel: 01768 88484

Dufton: Brow Farm, Dufton, Appleby CA16 6DB. Tel: 017683 52865

Dufton: Ghyll View, Dufton, Appleby CA16 6DB. Tel: 017683 51855

Garrigill: Post Office, Garrigill, Cumbria CA9 3DS. Tel: 01434 381257

Garrigill: East View, Garrigill, Cumbria CA9 3RS. Tel: 01434 381561

Kirkby Stephen: Fletcher House, Fletcher Hill, Kirkby Stephen CA17 4QQ. Tel: 017683 71013

Kirkoswald: The Fetherston Arms, Kirkoswald, Nr. Penrith CA10 1DQ. Tel: 01768 898284

Lazonby: Bracken Bank Lodge, Lazonby, Nr. Penrith CA10 1AX. Tel: 01768 898241

Long Marton: Broom House, Long Marton, Appleby-in-Westmorland CA16 6JP. Tel: 017683 61318

Maulds Meaburn: Meaburn Hill Farmhouse, Maulds Meaburn, Penrith CA10 3HN. Tel: 01931 715168

Milburn: Low Howgill Farm, Milburn, Penrith CA10 1TL. Tel: 017683 61595

Morland: Mill Beck Cottage, Morland CA10 3AY. Tel: 01931 714567

Nateby: The Black Bull Inn, Nateby, Kirkby Stephen CA17 4JP. Tel: 017683 71588

Newbiggin-on-Lune: Tranna Hill, Newbiggin-on-Lune, Kirkby Stephen CA17 4NY. Tel: 01539 623227

Outhgill: Ing Hill Lodge, Nr. Outhgill, Mallerstang Dale, Kirkby Stephen CA17 4JT. Tel: 017683 71153

Penrith: Corner House, 36 Victoria Road, Penrith CA11 8HR. Tel: 01768 863566

Ravenstonedale: Coldbeck House, Ravenstonedale, Kirkby Stephen CA17 4LW. Tel: 01539 623407

Sedbergh: Holmcroft, Station Road, Sedbergh LA10 5DW. Tel: 01539 620754

Wetheral: Killoran Country House Hotel, Wetheral, Cumbria Tel: 01228 560200

Also of Interest:

COME BACK TO EDEN: Lakeland's Northern Neighbour

John Hurst

A unique and absorbing account of one man's addictive love of this area of subtle beauty, it will appeal not only to Cumbrians but to all who enjoy the countryside. The author concentrates on the ebb and flow of life in town and country rather than the great and mighty. "Its leisurely and affectionate narrative and its vintage photographs remind us that the history of a nation is shaped not only by kings and politicians but also by ordinary men and women." – George Bott, *The Keswick Reminder. £7.95*

A LITERARY GUIDE TO THE LAKE DISTRICT

Grevel Lindop

A complete guide to the Lake District's literary connections from earliest times to the present day, illustrated and arranged in five easy-to-follow routes for walkers and drivers.

Recognised as a classic when first published, this is a fully revised and updated edition of an essential guide for all lovers of the Lake District.

The immense literary significance of this much loved National Park makes walking so much more interesting when you have at your fingertips such fascinating and detailed information.

Divided into five very user-friendly areas including the National Park and the Cumbrian coast, the guide is enhanced by specially-drawn maps and archive illustrations. *£10.95*

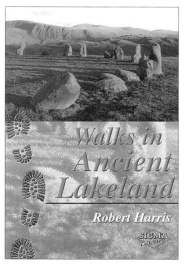

WALKS IN ANCIENT LAKELAND

Robert Harris

Enjoy a 'Walk in Ancient Lakeland' and discover sites and monuments from the Neolithic and Bronze Ages you never knew existed. Discover the great stone circles, standing stones and burial cairns which still decorate these beautiful hills. Follow the ancient trackways linking these ancient sites and explore largely unknown areas to uncover the mysteries of the lives of our ancestors in this timeless landscape. *£7.95*

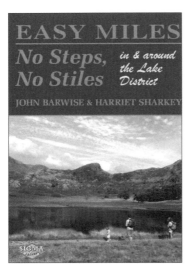

EASY MILES, NO STEPS NO STILES – IN & AROUND THE LAKE DISTRICT

Harriet Sharkey & John Barwise

Previously serialised in the *Westmorland Gazette*, **Easy Miles** features wonderful walks in and around the National Park, uninterrupted by steps or stiles. The routes are ideal for pushchairs, wheelchairs and anyone who just wants an easy stroll. Over 30 locations – some with spectacular views and others of special scientific or historical interest. Most routes include a pub, café or other refreshment point and many are accessible using public transport. *£7.95*

WALKING THE WAINWRIGHTS

Stuart Marshall

This ground-breaking book is a scheme of walks linking all the 214 peaks in the late Alfred Wainwright's seven-volume 'Pictorial Guide to The Lakeland Fells'. Route descriptions are clearly presented with two-colour sketch maps facing the descriptive text – so that the book can be carried flat in a standard map case. The walks average 12 miles in length but the more demanding ones are presented both as one-day and two-day excursions. *£7.95*

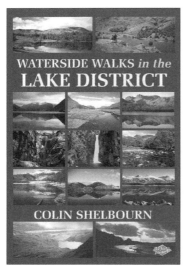

WATERSIDE WALKS IN THE LAKE DISTRICT

Colin Shelbourn

A unique compilation of 25 walks around and alongside a selection of the many water features to be found in this favourite walking area – lakes, tarns, becks, rivers and waterfalls. Ranging from 1 to 16 km, from gentle strolls to more strenuous hikes there are suitable walks for all age groups. Each walk includes information about parking, the length of the walk, a clear map to guide you, the level of difficulty, some very interesting facts of particular relevance and many beautiful photographs. *£7.95*